Terrorism & Extremism

Editor: Danielle Lobban

Volume 425

First published by Independence Educational Publishers

The Studio, High Green

Great Shelford

Cambridge CB22 5EG

England

© Independence 2023

Copyright

This book is sold subject to the condition that it shall not,
by way of trade or otherwise, be lent, resold, hired out or otherwise
circulated in any form of binding or cover other than that in which it
is published without the publisher's prior consent.

Photocopy licence

The material in this book is protected by copyright. However, the
purchaser is free to make multiple copies of particular articles for instructional
purposes for immediate use within the purchasing institution.
Making copies of the entire book is not permitted.

ISBN-13: 978 1 86168 885 9

Printed in Great Britain

Zenith Print Group

Acknowledgements

The publisher is grateful for permission to reproduce the material in this book. While every care has been taken to trace and acknowledge copyright, the publisher tenders its apology for any accidental infringement or where copyright has proved untraceable. The publisher would be pleased to come to a suitable arrangement in any such case with the rightful owner.

The material reproduced in **issues** books is provided as an educational resource only. The views, opinions and information contained within reprinted material in **issues** books do not necessarily represent those of Independence Educational Publishers and its employees.

Images

Cover image courtesy of iStock. All other images courtesy of Freepik and Unsplash.

Additional acknowledgements

With thanks to the Independence team: Shelley Baldry, Tracy Biram, Klaudia Sommer and Jackie Staines.

Danielle Lobban

Cambridge, May 2023

Contents

Chapter 1: Terrorism & Extremism Today

We need to talk about terrorism	1
Global Terrorism Index 2022: key findings in 6 charts	3
Ideology & psychology: where does extremism come from	6
Is left-wing or right-wing extremism more of a threat to Britain?	8
The disturbing rise of neo-Nazi terrorism in Britain	10
Boys under 15 are 'most at risk of radicalisation and turning to terrorism'	11
'I'm not afraid of terrorism. I'm afraid of being accused of being a terrorist': growing up Muslim after 9/11	12
Shamima Begum: who is the young woman seeking to have her British citizenship restored?	14
Why is deadly misogyny not recognised as a form of extremism?	16
Terror investigations at record high as threat of extreme right-wing 'lone actors' rises	18
Extremism in the UK: new definitions threaten human and civil rights	20
'I mean you no harm': from troubled teen to neo-Nazi footsoldier	22
The Dover bombings were a hate attack – why did it take so long to call them terrorism?	25

Chapter 2: Tackling Terrorism

Understanding and indentifying radicalisation risk in your education setting	27
Ministers studying plans for UK child-specific terrorism orders	29
Hate preachers to be held in 'jails within jails' to stop radicalisation of fellow inmates	31
UN Security Council boosts commitment to fight digital terror	32
Where next in the fight against Islamist extremism?	33
Terrorist recruitment now happens mainly online – which makes offenders easier to catch	35
Why dialogue is an essential tool for peace, security and development	36
Should we forgive extremists?	38
Inquiries differ on why the 2017 Manchester bombing wasn't prevented – here's why	40

Further Reading/Useful Websites	42
Glossary	43
Index	44

Introduction

Terrorism & Extremism is Volume 425 in the **issues** series. The aim of the series is to offer current, diverse information about important issues in our world, from a UK perspective.

About Terrorism & Extremism

Despite an increase in attacks, the number of deaths from terrorism continues to fall. This book considers different types of violent, extremist ideologies, where they come from and who is most at risk from radicalisation and recruitment. It also takes a look at the various strategies used to tackle terrorism...

Our sources

Titles in the **issues** series are designed to function as educational resource books, providing a balanced overview of a specific subject.

The information in our books is comprised of facts, articles and opinions from many different sources, including:

- Newspaper reports and opinion pieces
- Website factsheets
- Magazine and journal articles
- Statistics and surveys
- Government reports
- Literature from special interest groups.

A note on critical evaluation

Because the information reprinted here is from a number of different sources, readers should bear in mind the origin of the text and whether the source is likely to have a particular bias when presenting information (or when conducting their research). It is hoped that, as you read about the many aspects of the issues explored in this book, you will critically evaluate the information presented.

It is important that you decide whether you are being presented with facts or opinions. Does the writer give a biased or unbiased report? If an opinion is being expressed, do you agree with the writer? Is there potential bias to the 'facts' or statistics behind an article?

Activities

Throughout this book, you will find a selection of assignments and activities designed to help you engage with the articles you have been reading and to explore your own opinions. Some tasks will take longer than others and there is a mixture of design, writing and research-based activities that you can complete alone or in a group.

Further research

At the end of each article we have listed its source and a website that you can visit if you would like to conduct your own research. Please remember to critically evaluate any sources that you consult and consider whether the information you are viewing is accurate and unbiased.

Issues Online

The **issues** series of books is complemented by our online resource, issuesonline.co.uk

On the Issues Online website you will find a wealth of information, covering over 70 topics, to support the PSHE and RSE curriculum.

Why Issues Online?

Researching a topic? Issues Online is the best place to start for...

Librarians

Issues Online is an essential tool for librarians: feel confident you are signposting safe, reliable, user-friendly online resources to students and teaching staff alike. We provide multi-user concurrent access, so no waiting around for another student to finish with a resource. Issues Online also provides FREE downloadable posters for your shelf/wall/table displays.

Teachers

Issues Online is an ideal resource for lesson planning, inspiring lively debate in class and setting lessons and homework tasks.

Our accessible, engaging content helps deepen students' knowledge, promotes critical thinking and develops independent learning skills.

Issues Online saves precious preparation time. We wade through the wealth of material on the internet to filter the best quality, most relevant and up-to-date information you need to start exploring a topic.

Our carefully selected, balanced content presents an overview and insight into each topic from a variety of sources and viewpoints.

Students

Issues Online is designed to support your studies in a broad range of topics, particularly social issues relevant to young people today.

Thousands of articles, statistics and infographs instantly available to help you with research and assignments.

With 24/7 access using the powerful Algolia search system, you can find relevant information quickly, easily and safely anytime from your laptop, tablet or smartphone, in class or at home.

Visit issuesonline.co.uk to find out more!

Chapter 1: Terrorism & Extremism Today

We need to talk about terrorism

Today's progressive taboos around race and Islam are stifling constructive debate.

By Simon Cottee

When, earlier this month, a 16-year-old boy became Britain's youngest person to be convicted of terrorism offences, the British press responded with a mixture of disgust and incredulity, inquiring how someone so young could have become so fanatical. By all accounts, his career in violent extremism started at a remarkably early age: he joined a far-right internet forum when he was just 13. A year later, he had become a fully-fledged terrorist 'mastermind' running a 'Neo-Nazi cell' from his grandmother's house in Cornwall. The teen, who can't be named for legal reasons, had reportedly downloaded bomb-making manuals, spoke of his desire to launch a 'white jihad' and had recruited a 17-year-old British neo-Nazi who was convicted of preparing acts of terrorism last November.

The case of Britain's youngest ever terror offender is profoundly disturbing, reigniting serious concerns over young people and their vulnerabilities to radicalisation. But it also provides us with an opportunity to reflect on how we talk about terrorism, particularly in the highly politicised context of today's post-Trump world.

In a saner time, I suspect we would hesitate to call a 16-year-old who has not actually committed any acts of political violence a terrorist at all. The boy in question was convicted under the 'encouragement' and 'possession' instruments in British terrorism legislation (two and ten counts respectively). As serious as this is, it isn't terrorism as we conventionally understand it. It isn't, for example, the same as carrying out a suicide bombing at a pop concert, or beheading a school teacher.

But even if one accepts that possessing bomb-making manuals and sharing violently hateful messages on WhatsApp is terrorism, one would surely hesitate to call a disturbed and misguided 16-year-old who didn't realise he had recruited an undercover police officer a 'terrorist mastermind'. My colleague Keith Hayward, a professor of criminology at the University of Copenhagen in Denmark, has a word for this species of rhetorical slippage: adultification – the application of adult categories to those who are not yet adults. (Interestingly, the term is commonly used by sociologists to describe the racial bias against black schoolgirls in America, where they are unfairly viewed as more mature and 'less innocent' than their white counterparts.)

The sensationalisation of terrorism is, of course, nothing new. But the coverage of Britain's youngest 'terror teen' intimates at a decisive shift in reportorial protocols around terrorism. This shift doesn't reflect any real changes in the behaviour and threat level of terrorists, but is instead a direct consequence of the ever-tightening choke-hold of progressive taboos around race and Islam in contemporary western societies.

These taboos demand that we talk about terrorism in two distinct ways: on the one hand, we catastrophise its far-right variant, ramping up the agency and vileness of its perpetrators; while on the other, we infantilise its jihadi incarnation, playing down the agency of its instigators and forbidding any discussion of the religious motivations behind their violence.

As part of this juggling act, we are required to pretend that far-Right terrorism in America is far more problematic than jihadi extremism (this isn't to deny the significant recent uptick in lethal far-right terrorism in America). We are also asked to believe that while the ideology of the far-right is a primary driver of terrorism worldwide, the ideology of violent jihadism and its links to fringe interpretations of the Islamic faith has little or nothing to do with jihadi violence and conflict. This hypocrisy amounts to 'ideology for thee but not for me', as Graeme Wood has acidly put it.

Take, by way of illustration, the case of the three East London schoolgirls who left Britain in February 2015 to join ISIS in Syria. The response that followed was hysterical in many ways, but the girls and their families were given a mostly fair and lenient hearing. The consensus was that the girls – the youngest of whom, Shamima Begum, was 15 – were victims who had been 'groomed' by manipulative male online recruiters and bewitched by dangerously seductive ISIS propaganda.

For example, Sara Khan, the current head of the UK's Commission for Countering Extremism, wrote that 'just like child abusers groom their victims online and persuade them to leave their homes and meet them, male jihadists contact women through social media and online chatrooms, and build trust with them over time'. That consensus, however, was wrong. The real-life and online peer-groups in which they were radicalised were strictly women-only; the so-called online 'groomers' were in fact other ISIS-supporting women. And, of course, the vast majority of the pro-ISIS British girls were on the verge of womanhood, making the comparison to sexual grooming somewhat overblown. They may have been young, but it seems misguided to deny them any sense of agency.

Yet even when, aged 19, Begum surfaced in northern Syria and boasted to a reporter that seeing a severed head in a bin didn't really faze her – she told another that the Manchester Arena suicide bombing was justified – many liberals remained firmly in her corner, insisting that she was still a victim of grooming, and that she should be given a second chance.

This urge is noticeably less strong among progressives when it comes to far-Right terrorists. And I suspect this points to a politicisation of terrorism that makes it almost impossible to talk about it in a coherent and serious way.

Traditionally, the liberal-left consensus on terrorism was founded on three principles. The first concerned the fundamental illegitimacy of the word itself; it was, they said, simply a label used by the powerful to demonise and control the weak. It was a term and tool of repression, a way of legitimising the ever-widening net of social control against dissidents and rebels with a righteous cause.

The second part was concerned with the legitimacy of terrorism itself and the moral standing of the terrorist. While some – notably Leon Trotsky and Frantz Fanon – sought to brazenly justify 'red terror' as a weapon of the last resort in times of asymmetrical conflict, others were more equivocal, condemning the murder of innocents while at the same time making sure to situate such atrocities into a wider context that made it morally understandable ('This is wrong, but...'). From this perspective, the terrorist was not a monster, but instead a misguided soul who was 'pushed' or 'driven' to commit atrocious deeds. And whatever else he was, he was essentially forgivable; he was still one of us.

This is connected to a third and final aspect of this liberal-left consensus, which relates to the way that society should respond to acts of political violence. It took the form of the following cautionary wisdom: do not over-react to terrorism. Doing so not only tramples on human rights and sets in place a dangerous precedent for further rights-infringements, but it also risks alienating and further radicalising people, provoking a lethal 'blowback'.

Much of this worldview remains in place on the liberal-left, but in recent years it has been brought into conflict with the emergence of a second, contradictory consensus. According to this new paradigm, there is actually nothing wrong with the label 'terrorism'; what's wrong is that it's selectively applied to Muslims and other minority groups and not applied nearly enough to the white majority.

Moreover, the 'real' terrorists – whether they're storming the US Capitol or hiding on neo-Nazi online forums – really are monsters and deserve not an ounce of forgiveness. Indeed, they should be purged from the social order. And anyone who tries to contextualise or understand, still less give a platform to, these terrorists should be roundly condemned.

But the problem for liberal-leftists is that this consensus cannot co-exist with the other one. You can't implore forgiveness for Shamima Begum while at the same time scream for the metaphorical lynching of the Capitol rioters.

None of this would be much of a problem if the pathologies and contortions of the liberal-left's terrorism discourse simply remained there, but since this political tribe is now ascendant in elite institutions in America and parts of Europe, it's becoming a problem for the rest of us. Indeed, so culturally prevalent and deep are the progressive taboos around race and Islam in the West that it has become difficult to talk about terrorism in a sane and rational way. Even traditional centres of power – like the police and civil service – are seemingly incapable of talking plainly about the threats we face. Last summer, for instance, the Met Police considered dropping the term 'Islamist' when describing terror attacks carried out by jihadists.

Meanwhile, anyone who tries to understand the root causes of far-Right rancour is dismissed as a rank defender of the far-Right. The investigative journalist Naama Kates, for example, has told me that she regularly receives censure from so-called progressives for giving a platform to misogynistic 'involuntary celibates' on her superb Incel podcast; Kates's offence is that she uses a methodology called empathy to better understand incels.

Moreover, if you're not Muslim and study or report on jihadist violence, you run the risk of being accused of Islamophobia. Even Thomas Hegghammer, one of the world's leading experts on jihadism, has recently been accused of perpetuating 'stale and harmful notions of Muslim essentialism' – all because his focus on the conservative, non-violent and strongly religious cultural practices of otherwise violent Muslim militants is regarded as perpetuating a dangerous conflation between conservative Muslims and jihadists. Which is a bit like saying that if a person points out that Tommy Robinson eats dirty fry-ups, they are smearing all fry-up-eating Brits with the taint of white supremacy.

Plainly, this is nonsense. But it is also dangerous nonsense. The implication is that any reference to the Islamic religiosity of jihadists is off-limits. And the result, as we can see, is the creation of a schizoid terrorism discourse that leaves us dangerously ill-equipped to face common threats to peace and security.

We desperately need to better understand why and how people – from all backgrounds and faiths and ethnicities – embrace ideologies that command and license them to kill other people for political ends. And we must try to do so with an open mind and in a spirit of curious inquiry, accepting our findings wherever they lead. To abdicate this responsibility from fear of offending the shallow pieties of what John McWhorter calls 'the elect' is not only cowardly, but ultimately dangerous, given the very real threats that menace us.

22 February 2021

The above information is reprinted with kind permission from UnHerd.
© 2023 UnHerd

www.unherd.com

Global Terrorism Index 2022: key findings in 6 charts

A brief look at some of the key findings in the latest Global Terrorism Index 2022 report from the Institute for Economics and Peace.

Sub-Saharan Africa emerges as global epicentre of terrorism, as global deaths decline

The Global Terrorism Index 2022 report provides a comprehensive summary of the key global trends and patterns in terrorism over the last decade. The annual Global Terrorism Index, now in its ninth year, is developed by leading international think tank the Institute of Economics and Peace (IEP) and provides the most comprehensive resource on global terrorism trends.

Here are some of the key findings from the Global Terrorism Index 2022 in six charts.

1. Deaths from global terrorism continue to decline (Fig. 1)

The 2022 Global Terrorism Index (GTI) reveals that despite an increase in attacks, the impact of terrorism continues to decline. In 2021, deaths from terrorism fell by 1.2% to 7,142, while attacks rose by 17%, highlighting that terrorism is becoming less lethal. Two thirds of countries recorded no attacks or deaths from terrorism – the best result since 2007 – while 86 countries recorded an improvement on their GTI score. The number of deaths has remained approximately the same for the last four years.

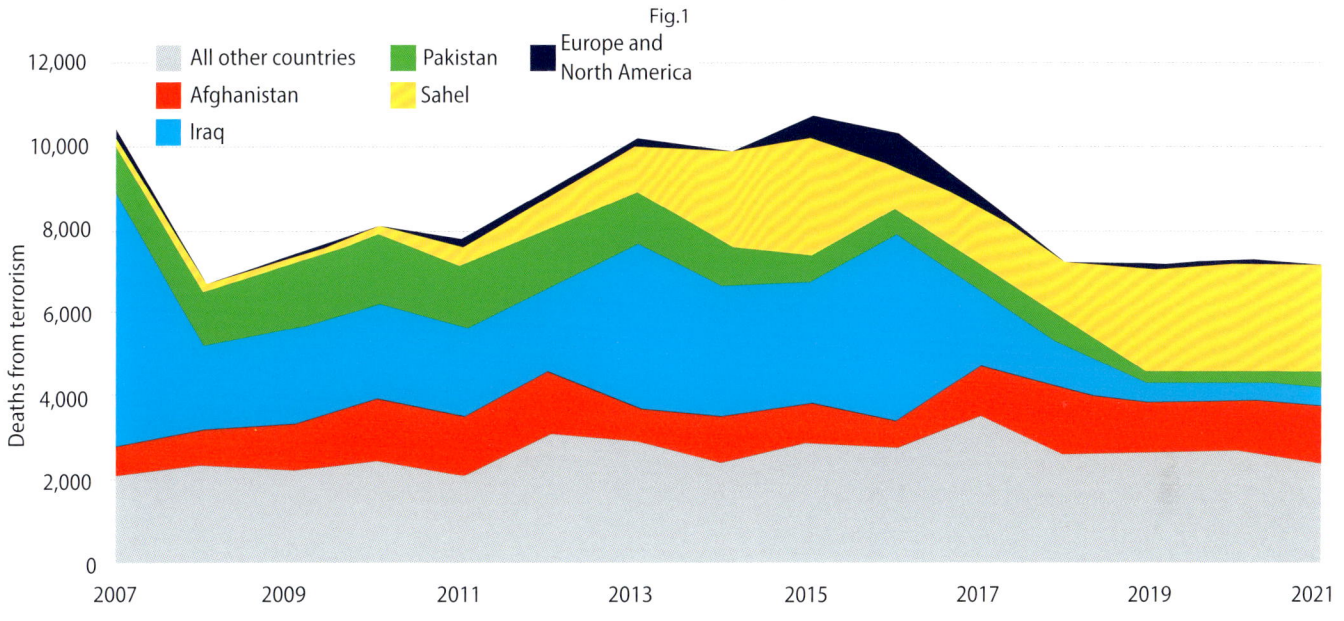

Source: Dragonfly Terrorism Tracker, IEP Calculations

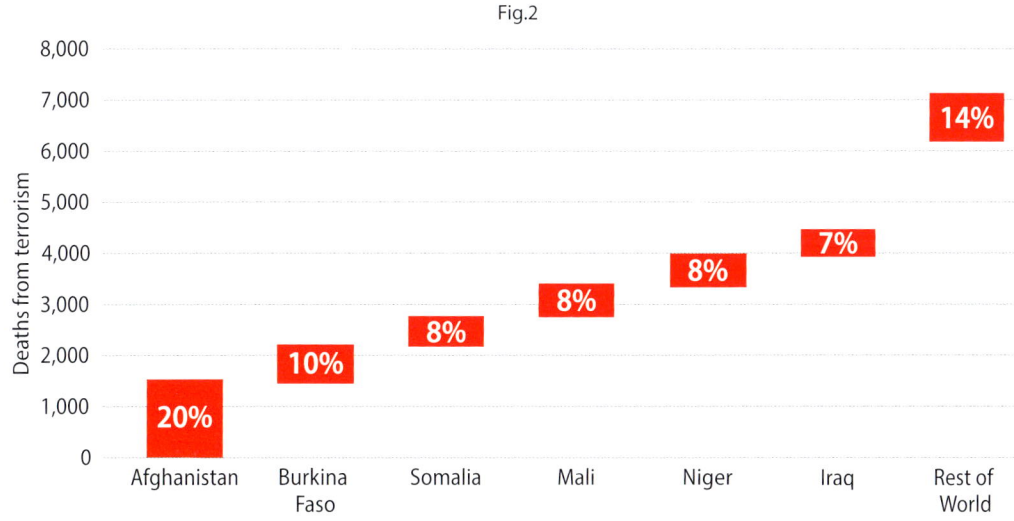

Source: Dragonfly Terrorism Tracker, IEP Calculations

2. Sub-Saharan Africa accounted for 48% of global terrorism deaths (Fig. 2)

The Index highlights that terrorism remains a serious threat, with Sub-Saharan Africa accounting for 48% of total global deaths from terrorism. Four of the nine countries with the largest increases in deaths from terrorism were also in sub-Saharan Africa: Niger, Mali, the DRC and Burkina Faso.

issues: Terrorism & Extremism   3   Chapter 1: Terrorism & Extremism Today

3. Sahel has become the new epicentre of terrorism (Fig. 3)

Following military defeats in Syria and Iraq, IS shifted its attention to the Sahel, with deaths from terrorism rising ten times in the region since 2007. The Sahel has become the new epicentre of terrorism. Terrorism in the region is compounded by high population growth, lack of adequate water and food, climate change and weak governments. Adding to the complexity, many criminal organisations are representing themselves as Islamic insurgencies.

4. In the West, politically motivated attacks overtook religious attacks, which declined by 82%. (Fig. 4)

In 2018, the number of deaths and incidents from political terrorism was higher than any other form for the first time since 2007. Political terrorism has increased steadily over the last decade, with 73 per cent of attacks in the West being attributed to politically motivated groups and individuals.

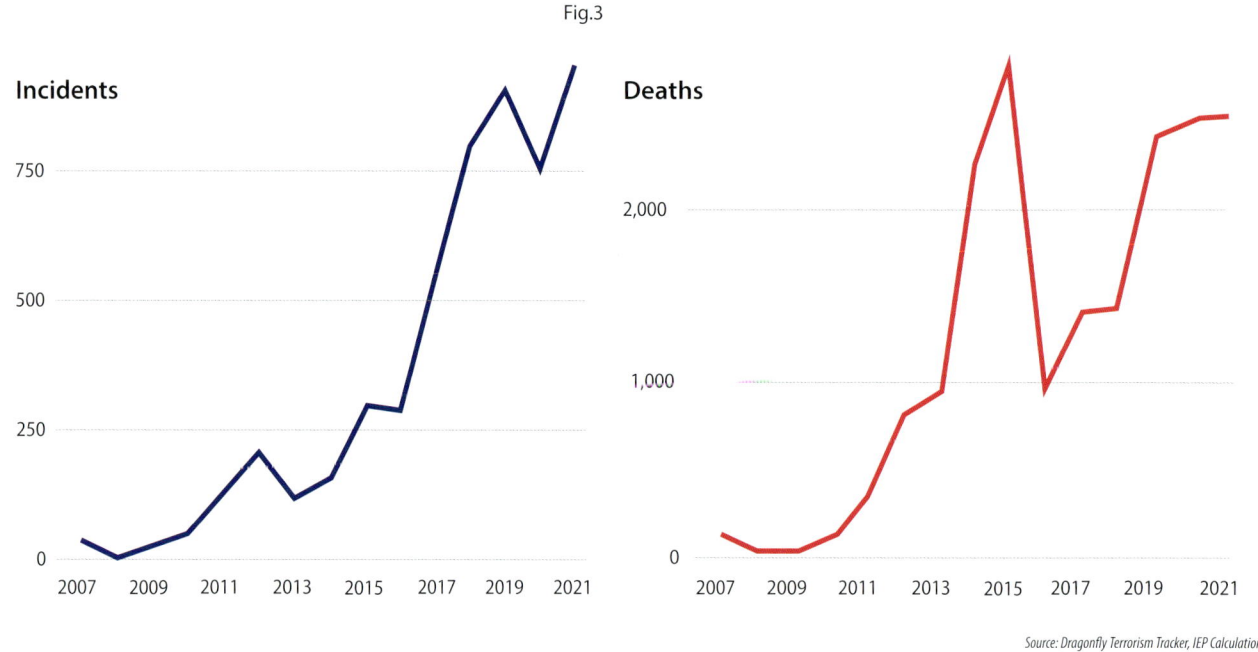

Source: Dragonfly Terrorism Tracker, IEP Calculations

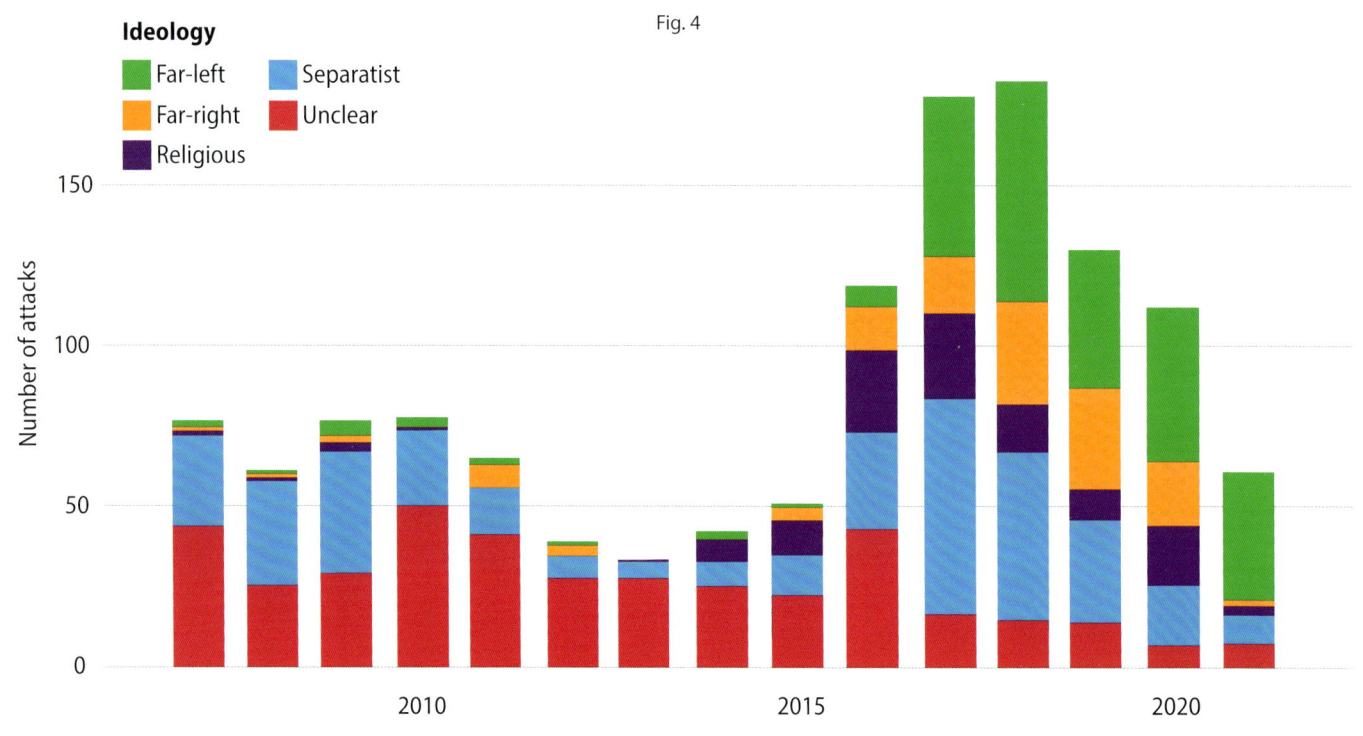

Source: Dragonfly Terrorism Tracker, IEP Calculations

Four deadliest terrorist groups in 2021

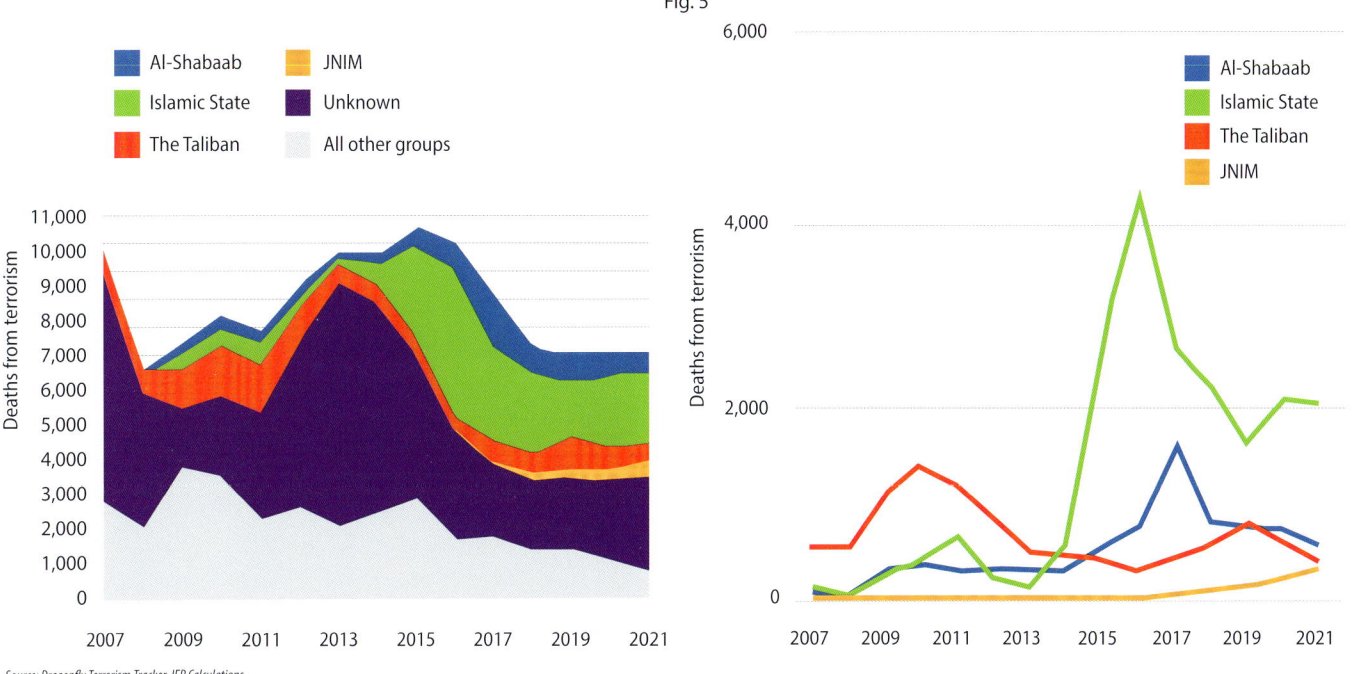

Fig. 5

GTI score, rank and change in score, 2011-2021

Fig. 6

Country	Average score	Change 2011-2021	Change 2020-2021
South Asia	5.559	-0.783	-0.203
North America	4.421	1.507	-0.298
Middle East and North Africa	3.547	-0.616	-0.294
South America	2.903	0.275	-0.049
sub-Saharan Africa	2.400	0.433	0.004
Asia-Pacific	2.045	-0.146	-0.219
Europe	1.368	-0.412	-0.284
Russia and Eurasia	0.876	-2.460	-0.405
Central America and the Caribbean	0.202	-1.132	-0.052

5. Islamic State (IS) replaces the Taliban as the world's deadliest terror group in 2021. (Fig. 5)

The four terrorist groups responsible for the most deaths in 2021 were Islamic State (IS), Al-Shabaab, the Taliban and Jamaat Nusrat Al-Islam wal Muslimeen (JNIM). These four groups were responsible for 3,364 deaths from terrorism, representing 47 per cent of total deaths in 2021.

Islamic State (IS) and its affiliate groups Islamic State – Khorasan Province (ISKP), Islamic State – Sinai Province (ISSP), and Islamic State in West Africa (ISWA) recorded the most attacks and deaths of any terrorist group in 2021. IS deaths represented 29 per cent of all deaths from terrorism globally in 2021.

6. The Ukraine conflict is likely to drive a rise in traditional and cyber terrorism. (Fig. 6)

Ukraine is likely to see an uplift in terrorism. In the 2014 crisis, the country recorded 69 terrorist attacks. Of serious concern are the knock-on effects of cyber terrorism to other countries. In addition to cyberattacks on the Ukraine, Russia has been credited with attacks on many other countries. It is possible that the threat of cyber terrorism will rise globally alongside the escalation of the Ukraine conflict.

The Ukraine conflict is likely to reverse gains in Russia and Eurasia, which recorded the largest improvement on the GTI in 2021, followed by North America.

2 March 2022

The above information is reprinted with kind permission from Institute for Economics & Peace
© 2023 Institute for Economics & Peace

www.visionofhumanity.org

Ideology & psychology: where does extremism come from?

CJ Werleman reports on a Cambridge University study which could shed new light on why some people support violence in the name of political or religious beliefs.

By CJ Werleman

When right-wing Americans stormed the United States Capitol to overthrow the Government they believed had stolen the 2020 Presidential Election from Donald Trump, the entire world watched aghast – wondering how so many people could become so easily radicalised into violence on provable lies.

We now might have the answer, thanks to new research conducted by the University of Cambridge, which has mapped an underlying 'psychological signature' for those predisposed to holding extremist views and supporting violence in the name of ideology, whether it be political, religious or otherwise.

'Although human existence is enveloped by ideologies, remarkably little is understood about the relationships between ideological attitudes and psychological traits,' observe the authors of the study. 'Even less is known about how cognitive dispositions – individual differences in how information is perceived and processed – sculpt individuals' ideological worldviews, proclivities for extremist beliefs and resistance (or receptivity) to evidence.'

Using an unprecedented number of cognitive tasks and personality surveys, along with data-driven analyses, the researchers discovered that a particular combination of personality traits and cognition – the way in which our brains perceive or process information – is a strong predictor for extremist views and dogmatism.

These traits include slower perceptual strategies ('the unconscious processing of changing stimuli, such as shape and colour'), poorer working memory and tendencies towards impulsivity and sensation seeking.

'This combination of traits – impulsivity in conjunction with slow and impaired accumulation of evidence from the decision environment – may result in the dogmatic tendency to discard evidence prematurely and to resist belief updating in light of new information,' the study states.

'Dogmatic participants were slower to accumulate evidence in speeded decision-making tasks but were also more impulsive and willing to take ethical risks.'

Certainly, new information and evidence matters not to the 70% of Republican voters who still believe Trump's Big Lie – which preceded the more than 30,000 documented lies he told before it – given that they continue to dismiss the findings of a dozen re-counts and Republican Party election officials, along with the rulings of 100 state and federal courts, including the Trump-stacked Supreme Court.

The study also found that political conservatives tend to be more vulnerable to 'dogmatism' and thus more resistant to evidence due to being more predisposed to 'cognitive caution' – described as 'slow-and-accurate unconscious decision-making', compared to fast-and-imprecise perceptual strategies found in those who tend to align with liberal political views.

The findings suggest that right-wing voters, nationalists and those with authoritarian impulses can be identified by reduced strategic information processing, heightened response caution in perceptual decision-making paradigms and aversion to social risk-taking, which, as the authors note, is consistent with numerous other studies that have linked right-wing ideologies with reduced analytical thinking and cognitive flexibility.

In 2012, researchers found that 'lower general intelligence in childhood predicts greater racism in adulthood, and this effect was largely mediated via conservative ideology', while a 1954 study found that those who hold extremist, right-wing views tend to be 'intolerant of ambiguity' and having an 'undue preference for symmetry, familiarity, definitiveness, and regularity; tendency toward black–white solutions, oversimplified dichotomising, unqualified either-or solutions, premature closure, perseveration and stereotypy'.

If that doesn't sound like Trumpism or right-wing-populism in a nutshell, then I'm not sure what does, particularly with regards to its hostility towards immigrants and proclivity for empty-headed slogans – 'Build the Wall', 'Lock Her Up', 'Stop the Steal'.

Dr Leor Zmigrod, one of the lead authors of the University of Cambridge study, found in earlier research that those who indicate strong attachment to a political party exhibit 'mental rigidity', relative to political moderates, and tend to see the world in black-and-white terms and 'struggle with new and different perspectives'.

'The more inflexible mind may be especially susceptible to the clarity, certainty, and safety frequently offered by strong loyalty to collective ideologies,' Dr Zmigrod told a science-based journal in 2019.

She has also found links between cognitive 'inflexibility' and pro-Brexit voters, observing that 'belief in rigid distinctions between the nationalistic in-group and out-group has

Brainstorm

In small groups, discuss what you know about extremism and extremist ideologies. List the different extremist movements you are aware of and consider the following:

- how do they communicate their cause?
- what are they trying to achieve?
- where in the world are they most active or dominant?

been a motivating force in citizens' voting behaviour', with more 'flexible' cognitive styles related to less nationalistic identities and attitudes.

Her newly-published study found that the psychological profile of individuals who endorse extreme pro-group actions, including violence against out-groups – remembering that roughly 30% of Republican voters expressed support for the attack on the Capitol – included a 'mix of the political conservatism signature and the dogmatism signature' which she and her co-authors believe offers 'key insights for nuanced educational programmes aimed at fostering humility and social understanding'.

Specifically, traits that make individuals more intellectually humble and receptive to evidence offer a counter to toxic ideologies and extremist rhetoric.

'There appear to be hidden similarities in the minds of those most willing to take extreme measures to support their ideological doctrines,' says Dr Zmigrod. 'Understanding this could help us to support those individuals vulnerable to extremism, and foster social understanding across ideological divides.'

The results of this study could not be more timely, given the domestic terrorist attack on the Capitol took place only months after the Department of Homeland Security assessed right-wing extremists and white supremacists to be 'the most persistent and lethal threat' to America, synching with an FBI warning that identified right-wing extremism to be a 'more urgent' threat than violent jihadism.

More research into why and how certain individuals are predisposed to holding extremist political views, including support of violence in the name of ideology, is urgently needed.

5 March 2021

Key Facts

- In January 2021 right-wing Americans stormed the United States Capitol to overthrow the Government they believed had stolen the 2020 Presidential Election from Donald Trump.
- Research conducted by the University of Cambridge, has mapped an underlying 'psychological signature' for those predisposed to holding extremist views and supporting violence in the name of ideology, whether it be political, religious or otherwise.
- In 2012, researchers found that 'lower general intelligence in childhood predicts greater racism in adulthood, and this effect was largely mediated via conservative ideology'.

The above information is reprinted with kind permission from Byline Times.
© 2023 Byline Media Holdings Ltd, Byline Times & Yes We Work Ltd

www.bylinetimes.com

Is left-wing or right-wing extremism more of a threat to Britain?

Right-wing radicals are seen as the more threatening than their left-wing opponents, but Islamic extremists are still seen as posing the biggest threat.

It has been reported that the government is ordering an investigation into both left-wing and right-wing extremist groups. The latest YouGov research shows that, of the two, right-wing extremists are more likely to be seen as a threat than their left-wing counterparts.

Some three in ten people (31%) think that right-wing extremists pose a 'big threat' while 23% say the same for left-wing extremists.

Among voting groups, respondents typically saw extremist groups at their end of the political spectrum as less of a 'big' threat, and those on the opposing end as more serious. For example, Labour (46%) and Lib Dem (49%) voters are twice as likely as Conservatives (22%) to see right-wing extremists as a 'big threat', while the Conservative perception of the threat posed by left-wing extremism is nearly three times greater than that of Labour voters (13%), and 19pts higher than Lib Dem supporters (17%).

Which extremist groups do Britons most see as a threat?

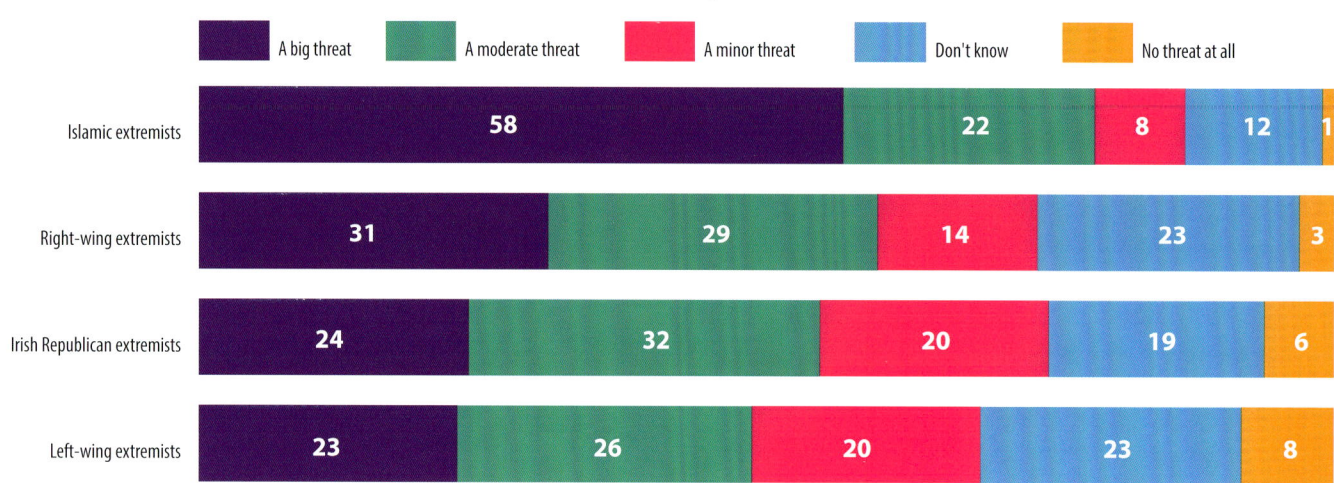

Islamic extremists are still seen as more of a threat than both right- and left-wing extremist groups

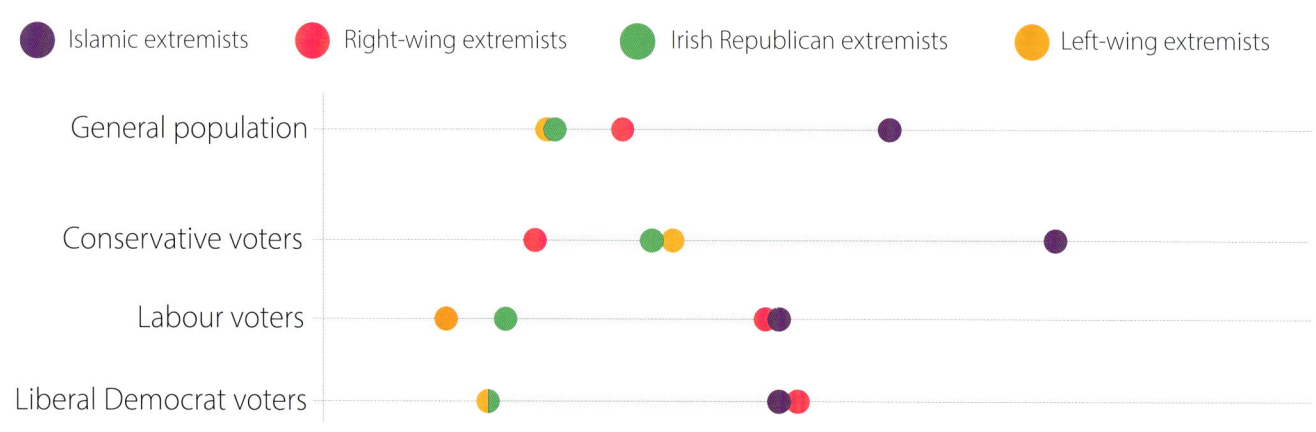

Source: YouGov - 17-18 February 2021

How should the government focus its investigation into left- and right-wing extremism?

The government has launched an investigation into both right-wing and left-wing extremism in the UK. Which of the two, if either, do you think should be the higher priority for the investigation to examine? % (Please note that this survey was conducted on the British mainland, i.e. in England Scotland and Wales, and so does not include Northern Irish respondents)

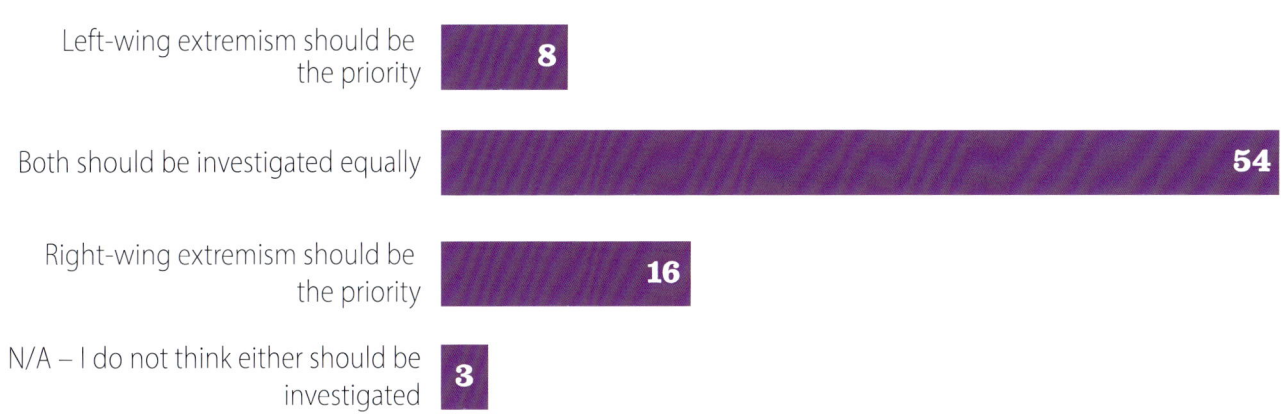

Source: YouGov - 17-18 February 2021

While a significant amount of people see these political extremists as threats, at 58% they are more likely to see Jihadists as a 'big threat' – around the same proportion who said that Islamic terror groups posed in big threat in a similar 2019 YouGov study.

Approaching a quarter of Britons (24%) also see Irish Republican groups as posing a 'big threat' putting them slightly ahead of left-wing extremists (23%) however is this within our margin of error.

While Conservatives see both groups as more of a threat than Labour and Lib Dem supporters, all three groups tend to see the threat posed by left-wing extremism to be around the same as that of Irish Republicans. Labour and Lib Dem voters, for their part, see the threat of right-wing extremists as being equally as serious as that of Jihadists,

How should the government focus its investigation into political extremism?

When it comes to the government's investigation into political extremism in the UK, half of Britons (54%) think it should focus on both ends of the spectrum equally. Some 8% of people think that left-wing extremism should be the priority for an investigation, but twice as many (16%) think it should focus more heavily on right-wing extremism.

A majority of both Conservative voters (62%) and Lib Dem voters (60%) think the investigation should cover both groups equally, while among Labour supporters this drops to 48% in favour of looking into both equally and 33% thinking it should weigh more heavily on right-wing extremism.

* Please note that this survey was only conducted on the British mainland, i.e. in England, Scotland and Wales, and so does not include Northern Irish respondents.

11 March 2021

The above information is reprinted with kind permission from YouGov.
© 2023 YouGov PLC

www.yougov.co.uk

The disturbing rise of neo-Nazi terrorism in Britain

By Ian Acheson

- 20% of terrorists in jail hold extreme right-wing beliefs
- In prison, the demand for status, meaning and money meets an unending supply of credulous young men
- White working class boys relegated to the margins of prosperity are vulnerable to online grooming

Neo-Nazis are the fastest growing cadre of violent extremists in our prisons, and now yet another offender motivated by far right ideology has entered our creaking jail system. Last week, Andrew Dymock was jailed for seven years for terrorist offences. Earlier this year Dymock, 24, was found guilty of multiple charges of encouraging and fundraising for terrorism. He was also convicted of possessing and disseminating terrorist material. He was unrepentant and the judge noted his 'calculated, sophisticated' behaviour designed to 'promote hatred and violence towards other human beings'. He was, the judge said, a 'leader, not a follower'.

Neo-Nazis make up 20% of the current prison terrorist population – 44 of the 215 terrorist offenders in custody at the last official count held extreme right-wing ideologies. The safeguarding strand of Britain's counter-terrorism strategy, Prevent, which evaluates those thought to be at risk of being drawn into extremism, is having record numbers of referrals from people suspected of holding far-right beliefs. Three quarters of young people between 18 and 21 arrested on suspicion of terrorist offences in the year to this April were far-right affiliated. The criminal justice conveyor belt seems crammed with white supremacists, many of whom, thwarted and isolated, have been either been radicalised by the internet or have used it to radicalise others.

Dymock will enter a prison system, probably at the top end in terms of his offence, which is already informally segregated in terms of power and space. Muslim prisoners are grossly over-represented in our jails, and they tend to form groups that share their religious characteristics. Some of these groups operate as gangs and, as we have seen in the recent case of the terrorist Usman Khan, these gangs exert control over everything from religious conversions to the illicit drugs market.

The emergence of far-right gangs is still largely the stuff of anecdote, but in places where space and control is contested and ideologues can mobilise people around the many grievances real or imagined that prison creates and magnifies, it is surely inevitable. Even those not drawn to such gangs will often make pragmatic decisions for their own safety to identify with them. Ideology of any stripe can provide a useful pretext for predators when the unending demand for status, meaning and money meets the unending supply of credulous young men.

The way to counter this phenomenon doesn't start with prison managers, always faced with playing the hand dealt by a rapacious criminal justice system and societal failure. But there is a clear responsibility on those running the system to ensure that people like Andrew Dymock – clearly a dangerous and charismatic 'leader' – are not permitted to mobilise others. Our prison system is a complex patchwork of potential recruits to or victims of violent extremism. Some groups, like veterans, making up around 2,800 people across the system could potentially be both. There is already some evidence that those most marginalised and vilified in custody, sex offenders, are being protected in exchange for converting to Islam. This is not normal. The number of far-right extremists who are also convicted of the possession of extreme child abuse pornography is another intriguing ingredient in the terrorist pathology that deserves further exploration. The number of occasions where people who have previous contact with prison custody go on to commit further offences of violent extremism is alarming.

The justified concern over Islamist extremist attacks with these factors in the background must be extended to extreme right-wing terrorists who will be just as determined to exploit their environment for gain, whether financial or ideological. Leaders like Andrew Dymock, adept at networking and grooming, who show no remorse for their crimes and who are able to intellectualise appalling racist ideologies, cannot be allowed the latitude to grow an insurgency in a system, shut down and overheated by Covid, that is barely capable of keeping the windows fixed.

Extreme right-wing terrorists will probably continue to grow as a proportion of the prison population. Eighteen months of lockdown, economic uncertainty, political turmoil, culture wars and the relegation of white working class boys to the margins of prosperity have all combined to create an explosion of online conspiracy theorists who are helping disenfranchised young men find a malign purpose in life. While we must be vigilant against those who would conflate the murderous potency of Islamist extremism with its mirror image on the extreme right, we cannot ignore the potential. In the southern US extreme right-wing gangs have made some prisons almost ungovernable. In Australia, biker gangs with neo-Nazi affiliations have become so dominant in jails, intimidating staff and controlling the narcotics trade, that they have their own separate prison, albeit rarely used in practice. Neo-Nazis in British jails are not yet strong enough or organised enough to compete with Islamists. But in places where mutual radicalisation is made ever easier by the withdrawal of legitimate authority, and warped perceptions can be honed by dangerous propagandists like Andrew Dymock, there can be no room for complacency. We need a strategy. I don't know if it exists.

27 July 2021

Professor Ian Acheson is a former prison officer and Senior Advisor to the Counter Extremism Project.

The above information is reprinted with kind permission from CAPX
© CENTRE FOR POLICY STUDIES 2023

www.capx.co

Boys under 15 are 'most at risk of radicalisation and turning to terrorism'

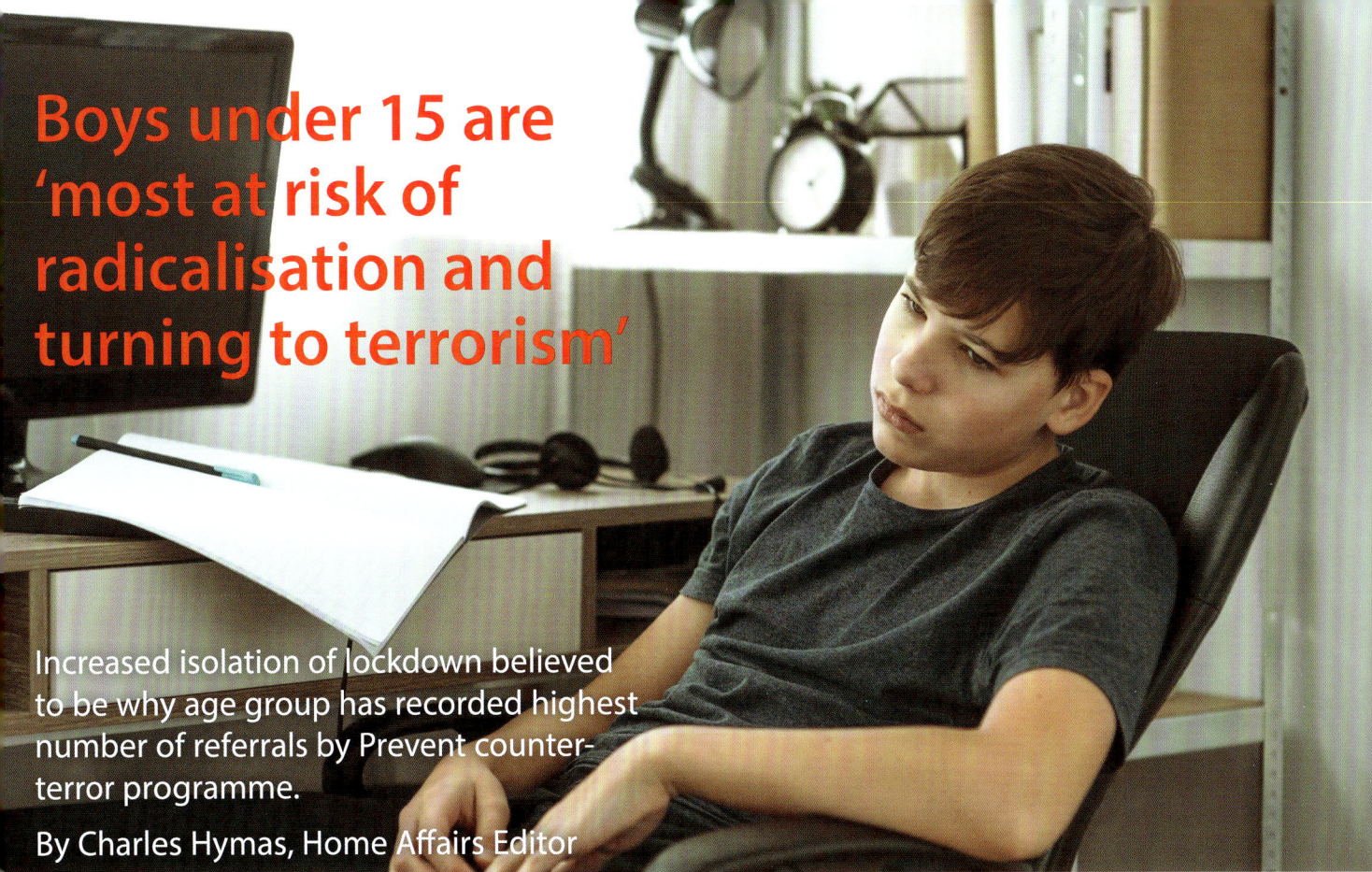

Increased isolation of lockdown believed to be why age group has recorded highest number of referrals by Prevent counter-terror programme.

By Charles Hymas, Home Affairs Editor

Schoolchildren aged under 15 accounted for the highest proportion of people deemed by the Government's Prevent counter-terrorism programme to be most at risk of radicalisation, figures have revealed.

Under-15s, predominantly boys, formed the largest of any age group to be referred on by Prevent to so-called Channel programmes, designed for those judged to be most at risk of radicalisation and turning to terrorism.

They contributed to a 30 per cent rise – to 6,406 – in the number of people referred to Prevent in the year to March 2022. Experts suggested the rise was fuelled by the Covid lockdowns, when more children could have been exposed to extremism as they went online whilst away from school and potentially isolated from friends.

The Home Office figures showed under-15s made up 1,829 – or 29 per cent – of the referrals to Prevent, with 299 adopted by Channel officials. That accounted for 37 per cent of all such cases and ahead of the previous top group of 15 to 20-year-olds.

Education provided the highest number of referrals to the Prevent programme for the first time, at 2,305 or 36 per cent – overtaking police, who referred 1,808, or 28 per cent.

Review expected to criticise Prevent

The figures, published on Thursday, come as the Government prepares to publish its long-awaited review of Prevent by historian and author William Shawcross, the former chairman of the Charity Commission.

It is expected to criticise Prevent for straying from its 'core mission' of stopping people from becoming terrorists by putting too much emphasis on treating them as victims.

It is also expected to say that Prevent is 'out of kilter' with the rest of the counter-terrorism system by focusing on Right-wing extremism at the expense of the Islamist threat, which accounts for the vast majority of terror attacks.

The vast majority – 89 per cent, or 5,725 – were male, rising to 92 per cent of those referred on to Channel. Extreme Right-wing radicalisation accounted for 1,309, or 20 per cent, and Islamist ideology for 16 per cent, or 1,027.

Two per cent – 154 – of referrals were due to concerns regarding school massacres, and one per cent – 77 – of concerns were incel-related, an online community of young men who consider themselves unable to attract women sexually and turn to hostility.

Lockdowns could have fuelled extremism

Ian Acheson, a former prison governor who led an independent review of Islamist extremism in jails, said the increase could be explained by children being kept away from school and friends by lockdowns.

'It is probably no surprise that they have been looking at things that are inappropriate, raising suspicions in those close to them that they are being drawn into extremism,' he said.

There was also evidence suggesting some of those referring people to Prevent were unclear about the requirements of the programme. The data suggested the largest number of referrals at a third of the total, 2,127, related to people 'with a vulnerability present but no ideology or counter-terrorism risk'.

26 January 2023

The above information is reprinted with kind permission from *The Telegraph*.
© Telegraph Media Group Limited 2023

www.telegraph.co.uk

'I'm not afraid of terrorism. I'm afraid of being accused of being a terrorist': growing up Muslim after 9/11

An article from The Conversation.
By Randa Abdel Fattah, DECRA Research Fellow, Macquarie University

Those born after 2001 have only known a world 'at war on terror'.

This means a generation growing up under fears and moral panics about Muslims and unparalleled security measures around their bodies and lives.

In my new book, *Coming of Age in the War on Terror*, I look at what this has meant for young Muslims in Australia as they navigate their political identities at school.

An impact on everyday life

In 2018 and 2019, I interviewed and held writing workshops with over 60 Muslim and non-Muslim high school students across Sydney who were born around the time of the September 11 terror attacks. We explored their fears, their levels of trust with peers and teachers and political expression in a post 9/11 world.

No matter how many Muslim students spoke to me about their typically adolescent hobbies and interests, almost every student spoke about the impact of political and media discourse in their everyday lives. Abdul-Rahman, a 17-year-old Muslim boy at an Islamic school in western Sydney, put it this way:

> 'I'm not afraid of terrorism. I'm afraid of being accused of being a terrorist.'

Another student, Laila, told me:

> 'I've always had this almost preconceived guilt attached to me [...] [It's] the million messages in the media, politicians, popular culture, all these little things that add up and add up.'

'Countering violent extremism'

For teenagers to talk about themselves as potentially 'accused' is devastating, but not particularly surprising.

For two decades, millions of federal and state dollars have been poured into 'countering violent extremism' programs targeting Muslim youth. There has been no subtlety here. Counter-terrorism policies have been announced by politicians on the steps of mosques, with a focus on geographic and demographic populations deemed 'at risk' (in other words, suburbs with large Muslim populations).

Consultations and round tables with government over 'national security' have been highly publicised. Meanwhile, Islamophobic attacks have been condemned by politicians and the police because of how they might 'undermine' relationships of cooperation between intelligence and law enforcement and the Muslim community.

Meanwhile, the public has been routinely reassured the government is tackling the 'problem' of young Muslim Australians, 'with strong, deradicalisation programs, working with Muslim communities'.

The figure of the vulnerable but also dangerous Muslim youth pops up time and time again, from moral panics around young 'homegrown' terrorists, to attempts to introduce 'jihadi watch' schemes in schools.

The pressure to self-censor

This landscape trickles down into young people's everyday lives, including their schools.

The pressure to self-censor and manage your political and religious expression at school was a common theme among many students, resonating with what academics in the United Kingdom describe in their research.

Anticipating how their tone, words and emotion would be interpreted by teachers and peers restricted students' political expression.

This included a young Palestinian girl who had to push back against teachers, who reprimanded her for wearing a 'Free Palestine' t-shirt at school, to students who refrained from writing about Iraq or Afghanistan as part of assignments because they had been cautioned not to 'bring overseas conflicts into the classroom'.

Other students talked of staying quiet if controversial topics came up in class, such as news of a terrorist attack involving Muslims, or media headlines about Islam. I also met students who tried to appear as 'good' or 'moderate' Muslims (which inevitably meant apolitical) and erased all traces of their Muslimness to 'fit in'.

Feeling targeted, isolated

In 2015, there was a media frenzy about youth radicalisation in prayer rooms in Sydney's state schools. I interviewed students at a school in north-west Sydney three years later and they spoke about how that controversy had been felt in their school life.

Most of the students from suburbs and schools who came under media and political scrutiny as 'problematic' had felt targeted and isolated. One student withdrew from his Muslim peers, abandoned his prayers at school, took different routes to school to avoid being hassled by the media, and 'shut down' in class.

> 'I got dragged into an argument with other kids in class about me following the same religion as these terrorists [...] but my tone [...] I came off very aggressive [...] then I was scared, because that's what people think of as radical extremists [...] I felt like I'd be taken straight to the principal and you would have to deal with that. So I shut up.'

We need a new approach

After two decades of seeing young Muslims as 'problems' to be contained and managed, it is time we approached them in a different way.

Adolescence is a time to encourage critical thinking and support young people navigating their political identities and agency. Young people need to be empowered to work through their political and religious ideas and identities in safe, supportive environments. They need to be seen as individuals in their own right, not members of a demonised, racialised collective.

The vast majority of the young Muslims I spoke to were matter-of-fact about the global rise of Islamophobia and racism. They knew about certain jokes and assumptions in the popular vernacular (for example, 'Allahu Akbar and bomb jokes' or 'terrorist' equals 'Muslim').

Many were concerned about what this meant as they grew up and left school. They worried about facing discrimination at work and being able to practise their faith openly. They also knew how this suspicion and dehumanisation had been triggered by wider discourses and policies over which they had no power.

It is not up to the 9/11 generation to change this. We need teachers, politicians and the media to create a culture where young Muslims feel accepted and secure in their right to express their religious and political identities.

5 September 2021

THE CONVERSATION

The above information is reprinted with kind permission from The Conversation.
© 2010-2023, The Conversation Trust (UK) Limited

www.theconversation.com

Shamima Begum: Who is the young woman seeking to have her British citizenship restored?

Mother who fled Britain as a schoolgirl to join terrorist militants in Syria has since appealed for forgiveness and argued she has been left 'stateless'.

By Joe Sommerlad

Shamima Begum is set to begin her appeal against the decision to revoke her British citizenship on national security grounds.

A Special Immigration Appeals Commission (SIAC) hearing to consider her case opens on Monday at Field House tribunal centre in London and is expected to last for five days.

Ms Begum, now 23, was raised in east London by parents of Bangladeshi origin and attended Bethnal Green Academy but, as a 15-year-old schoolgirl, fled for Syria via Turkey in February 2015 alongside two friends – Kadiza Sultana and Amira Abase – in order to join the Isis terrorist faction then engaged in regular attacks on European capitals and seizing territory in the Middle East.

British counter-terrorism police launched an international manhunt to find the trio but to no avail.

Ms Begum lived with the Islamist extremists for more than three years, marrying Dutch convert Yago Riedijk 10 days after arriving in Syria, a convicted terrorist with whom she had at least three children, two of whom died in infancy of malnutrition.

Riedijk, now held in a Syrian detention centre but originally from Arnhem, has since described their 'beautiful' life together and happy times baking cakes, even telling filmmaker Alan Duncan of his hope that they might 'start a family again' in the Netherlands.

Driven from Raqqa in October 2017 when US-backed fighters regained control of the city, Ms Begum was subsequently found on 13 February 2019 by Anthony Lloyd, war correspondent to The Times.

She was nine months pregnant with a baby boy at the time and living at the al-Hawl refugee camp in northern Syria, at which point her UK passport was withdrawn by then-home secretary Sajid Javid on the basis that she continued to pose a threat to Britain and was in a position to seek alternative citizenship in Bangladesh because of her parents' heritage.

'My number one job is to do whatever I can to keep this country safe,' Mr Javid said, explaining his decision.

Sajid Javid says he made 'absolutely the right decision' on Shamima Begum.

UK law allows the government to remove citizenship if they can show the person concerned behaved 'in a manner which is seriously prejudicial to the vital interests of the UK' and when there is 'reasonable grounds for believing that the person is able, under the law of a country or territory outside the UK, to become a national of such a country or territory.'

Ms Begum denied any involvement in the Islamist group's terror campaign and has attempted to challenge the Home Office's decision since April 2019 on the basis that it risks leaving her 'stateless' and potentially exposed to the risk of death or inhuman and degrading treatment.

On 16 July 2020, the UK Court of Appeal ruled that 'the only way in which she can have a fair and effective appeal is to be permitted to come into the United Kingdom to pursue her appeal'.

On reaching that decision, Lord Flaux said: 'Fairness and justice must, on the facts of this case, outweigh the national security concerns, so that the leave to enter appeals should be allowed.'

Ms Begum and the Home Office were then invited to present their arguments to the Supreme Court, the UK's highest legal authority, while the applicant was then living at another camp, al-Roj, in northeastern Syria in conditions her lawyers' described as 'dire'.

Ms Begum said she was 'very happy' but 'very nervous' about the prospect of returning to Britain, expressing concern 'about what will happen to her and how people will look at her there'.

That prospect failed to come to pass, however, as the Supreme Court's panel of five justices, led by Lord Reed, ruled on 26 February 2021 that she would not be allowed leave to enter the UK to pursue her appeal after all.

During an interview on ITV's Good Morning Britain on 15 September 2021, Ms Begum appealed for forgiveness from the British people and said she wanted to be brought back to the UK to face charges, adding in a direct appeal to then-prime minister Boris Johnson that she could be 'an asset' in the fight against terror.

She insisted she had been 'groomed' as a 'dumb kid' and radicalised by propaganda videos seen online.

Walking back remarks previously made to a BBC journalist about the Manchester Arena bombing of 2017 when she said that Isis considered the killings 'justified' in light of the airstrikes being carried out against them, she said: 'I do not believe that one evil justifies another evil. I don't think that

Key Facts

- As a 15-year-old schoolgirl, fled for Syria via Turkey in February 2015 alongside two friends – Kadiza Sultana and Amira Abase – in order to join the Isis terrorist faction.
- Ms Begum had her UK citizenship removed by the Home office in February 2019 rendering her 'stateless'.
- Ms Begum's request to be allowed to enter the UK to appeal the Home Office's decision was refused by the Supreme Court in February 2021.
- Ms Begum's most recent challenge to the deprivation of her British citizenship was dismissed in February 2023. Her lawyers plan to appeal the decision at the Court of Appeal.

women and children should be killed for other people's motives and for other people's agendas.'

Tasnime Akunjee, a lawyer for the Begum family, said in a statement ahead of Monday's hearing: 'Shamima Begum will have a hearing in the SIAC court, where one of the main arguments will be that when former home secretary Sajid Javid stripped Shamima Begum of her citizenship leaving her in Syria, he did not consider that she was a victim of trafficking.

'The UK has international obligations as to how we view a trafficked person and what culpability we prescribed to them for their actions.'

That argument relates to the role played in her decision to flee by Mohammed al-Rasheed, an Isis fixer who is alleged by the BBC and *The Times* to have been a double agent also working for the Canadian government and who is thought to have met the girls in Turkey before taking them on to Syria in 2015.

As for what happened to Ms Begum's companions, Ms Sultana was reportedly killed in a Russian air raid while Ms Abase is still missing, although it has been claimed that she is still in Syria.

Additional reporting by agencies

21 November 2022

Discuss

The case of Shamima Begum has received an enormous amount of media attention over the last couple of years. Opinion is divided on whether or not she should have her British citizenship reinstated and be allowed to return to the UK. Discuss as a class the reasons for both sides of the argument. Write up a summary of the discussion.

The above information is reprinted with kind permission from *The Independent*.
© independent.co.uk 2023

www.independent.co.uk

Why is deadly misogyny not recognised as a form of extremism?

The Plymouth shooting is a perfect illustration of the failure of the UK's counter-terrorism apparatus to fully understand emerging threats, argues Dr Maria Norris.

By Dr Maria Norris

'It is a different sort of ideology'. This was the way in which Jonathan Hall QC, the Independent Reviewer of Terrorism Legislation, described the recent shooting in Plymouth, which saw Jake Davison kill five people including his mother and a three-year-old girl, before taking his own life.

It has now emerged that the killings may be reclassified as a terror attack, after initially being described as a 'domestic incident'. However, comments like Hall's suggest that there is still much cause for concern.

Hall argued that the shooting 'fits rather uneasily into the way the authorities understand ideologies' and 'seems part of right-wing terrorism but it is not really. In fact, it is quite separate from it'.

Such comments are illustrative of a fundamental problem at the core of the UK's counter-terrorism apparatus: its failure to grapple with, and fully understand, the emerging threat from extreme misogyny and far-right extremism.

The significance of misogyny

The failure to understand the ideological underpinnings of the Plymouth shooting betrays an old-fashioned and outdated way of looking at terrorism.

The threat is no longer only emanating from formal groups with distinct symbols and membership, it is now far more nebulous – emerging from diaphanous online communities which are more dangerous precisely because of their non-corporeality.

It is true that there is no formal 'incel' organisation equivalent to far-right groups such as Sonnenkrieg Division or National Action. But formal-right right groups themselves only represent a very small percentage of far-right extremists.

Andres Behring Breivik, responsible for the 2011 Norway attacks; Dylan Roof, of the Charleston Church shooting; and Brenton Harrison Tarrant, the Christchurch mosque shooter, did not belong to any formal extremist group. Neither did Thomas Mair, the neo-nazi who murdered Labour MP Jo Cox in 2016.

Hall's insistence that extreme misogyny is a 'different sort of ideology', separate from far-right extremism, is simply inaccurate. As Sian Norris argues, at the core of both incels and the far-right is a belief in the fascistic natural order of white male supremacy. The incel ideology relies on the belief of the inherent superiority of the white male, while far-right ideology is steeped in extreme misogyny. One cannot be separated from the other, and yet, they often are in the eyes of the law.

As Joan Smith also argues, the significance of extreme misogyny at the roots of a fatal attack is often missed. James Alex Fields Jr was a far-right extremist who ploughed his van into the crowd during the Unite the Right rally in Charlottesville, Virginia, in 2017, killing Heather Heyer. It is an established fact that Fields Jr is a white supremacist. But what is less well known is that he was chanting 'white Sharia now', a popular incel slogan, as he drove into the crowd.

Two years later, in 2019, two teenage neo-nazis were jailed in London for terrorist offences. What was not part of the coverage was the fact that they also advocated for the mass rape of women. Both Darren Osbone and Khaled Masood, who committed the 2017 attacks on the Finsbury Park Mosque and Westminster bridge respectively, had a history of abusing women.

Racialised definitions

It is disconcerting to see both the Independent Reviewer of Terrorism Legislation and law enforcement agencies get this so wrong. But those tasked with our national security have been getting it wrong for a long time.

For two decades, the label of 'terrorism' has been deployed in a racially selective manner. The Plymouth shooting is just the latest deadly example of a violent action meeting the criteria set out under the legal definition of terrorism, and yet not being considered as an act of terror.

In 2013, the brutal murder of Drummer Lee Rigby by two Islamic extremists was immediately portrayed as terrorism by the Government and the media. On the day after the killing, the then Prime Minister David Cameron proclaimed that Britain would 'be absolutely resolute in its stand against violent extremism and terror' and then announced the creation of a new taskforce to tackle extremism.

But a series of retaliatory attacks on Muslim communities which started soon after Drummer Rigby's murder went unremarked – even though most neatly fell under the legal definition of terrorism as stated in the Terrorism Act 2000.

Key Facts
- Incel and far-right ideologies believe in the fascistic natural order of white male supremacy.
- The Terrorism Act was passed by UK parliament in 2000

Not even the murder of Mohammed Saleem by a far-right extremist in the same year was considered an act of terror.

The two decades since the inception of the Terrorism Act 2000 have seen the might of counter-terrorism powers unleashed disproportionately on the Muslim community, causing untold damage. At the same time, other forms of extremism continued to grow – mostly under the radar.

As Laura Bates argues in her book *Men Who Hate Women*: 'What if we can't begin to take a comprehensive and effective approach to policing acts of violence, because we don't describe them in the ways that acknowledge the connections between them? What if our ideas about men and women, about misogyny and hate crime, about what terrorists look like, are so trapped in stereotypes that we are making terrible mistakes?'

Jake Davison had his firearms licence returned in December after agreeing to take part in an anger management course. If the connections between extreme misogyny and the far-right were acknowledged, then would he even have been in possession of a shotgun last week? As Joan Smith aptly reminds us, the Manchester Arena bomber previously avoided a referral to the Prevent counter-terrorism programme after owning up to anger management issues.

How many atrocities could have been prevented if extreme misogyny was taken seriously as a threat, or at the very least, as a warning sign? How long until another angry man, radicalised in online forums of hate, picks up a weapon and opens fire?

Too many times we have seen the devastating end results of an insidious cycle of radicalisation – a cycle still being overlooked by the authorities due to the glaring failings of the UK's counter-terrorism strategy.

18 August 2021

Write

Write a one-paragraph definition of each of the following terms:
- Incel
- Misogyny
- White male supremacy

The above information is reprinted with kind permission from BYLINE TIMES
© 2023 Byline Media Holdings Ltd, Byline Times & Yes We Work Ltd

www.bylinetimes.com

Terror investigations at record high as threat of extreme right-wing 'lone actors' rises

MI5 and counter terrorism police are looking into 800 potential threats as 'lone actors' influenced by online hate.

By David Parsley, Chief News Correspondent 28 December 2022

UK security services are investigating a record number of potential terror threats following a rise in right-wing extremism, *i* can reveal.

The scale of the extreme right-wing terrorist threat has steadily increased over the past 20 years, and is believed to be largely posed by young people influenced by social media and online sites.

Counter terrorism police and MI5 are engaged in more than 800 investigations, the highest since such records began to be kept in 2002 after the 9/11 attacks, and there is no sign that the intensity will drop in the near future.

Isis, al-Qaeda and other Islamist terrorist groups remain the highest threat, but the rise in right-wing extremism has been particularly strong since the EU Referendum in 2016, with the cost of living crisis, the Channel migrants issue and the post-Brexit era cited as leading causes.

Tracking down would-be terrorists is particularly difficult because so many are 'lone actors' who are inspired to act independently rather than as part of a wider organisation.

Security services have, they say, foiled eight imminent terror attacks since the summer of 2021, and 37 since 2017. Around a third are linked to right-wing extremists.

A spokeswoman for Counter Terrorism Policing (CTP) said: 'Along with our colleagues in the security services, we have disrupted 37 late stage terror plots since 2017, eight since summer 2021.

'We are currently working on a record number of more than 800 investigations, the majority of which are in partnership with our colleagues at MI5. These investigations encompass a range of activities, including fund-raising, possession and dissemination offences and preparing acts of terrorism.

'Our increasing casework in this area is believed to be driven by rising numbers of young people being drawn into the ideology, through social media and online platforms.'

In April 2020, MI5 took control over the monitoring for what the domestic security service describes as 'extreme right-wing terrorism and left, anarchist and single issue terrorism'.

The CTP spokeswoman added: 'The primary manifestation of the threat in the UK is via self-initiated terrorists, individuals with no assistance from extreme right-wing terrorist groups.

'At CTP we are increasingly concerned about the radicalisation of young people in this space, and are working hard to put interventions in place, to stop them taking this path.'

The rise of extreme right-wing ideologies was blamed for the firebombing of an immigration processing centre in Dover on 30 October.

Andrew Leak, 66, killed himself after throwing incendiary devices into the Western Jet Foil site in the port city. The attack injured two people and more than 700 migrants had to be relocated.

- MI5 currently working on record 800-plus terror investigations
- 37 'late stage' plots foiled since 2017, eight imminent threats since summer 2021
- CTP says 'increasing casework driven by rising numbers of youth drawn into the ideology through social media and online platforms'
- Police are 'increasingly concerned about the radicalisation of young people' to right-wing causes
- Former counter terror chief tells *i* that crowded spaces, sporting and entertainment venues, and politicians at risk
- MI5 seeks access to encrypted messaging services, given that extremists tend to use encrypted platforms and virtual private networks
- Extreme right-wing terror threats have increased to such a level that they now form part of the overall UK Threat Level assessment

CTP recovered evidence that suggested Leak was motivated by extreme right-wing ideology.

In June, the co-founder of secretive right-wing group National Action, Alex Davies, was sentenced to eight years and six months in prison after being convicted of being a member of a proscribed organisation.

National Action was jointly founded by Davies in 2013 but joined the list of extremist groups proscribed by the government in December 2016 after it drew greater attention to itself by openly celebrating the murder of Jo Cox MP.

Topping the list of feared attacks are lone actors building crude homemade improvised explosive devices, similar to that used in the Admiral Duncan attack in London in 1999, intelligence sources told *i*. Known as one of Soho's oldest gay pubs, it was the site chosen by neo-Nazi David Copeland to detonate a nail bomb which killed three people and left more than 70 injured.

There is a high level of concern that individuals plotting attacks are far more difficult to gather intelligence on compared to organised terror groups, either within or outside the UK.

The risk of attacks on crowded city centre leisure districts, sporting and entertainment venues have also increased, according to one former counter terrorism chief.

Nick Aldworth, who was the national co-ordinator at CTP until 2019, said: 'The right-wing has been the fastest growing threat in the UK for the last couple of years.

'Right-wing terrorists have a history of being lone actors and I don't see anything to suggest that they are organised as groups. It is, however, symptomatic of generally declining social stability and there is research to suggest that at such times, terrorism grows.

'The greatest threat globally – in terms of quantum – from terrorism is currently against political targets rather than crowds, but in the UK it has manifested itself against a range of targets including crowds, private gatherings and political targets.'

In June 2016, Labour MP Jo Cox was murdered by a right-wing extremist Thomas Mair during the Brexit Referendum campaign.

As a result of the growing threat, MI5 has called on communications service providers to allow the security agency to have exceptional access to encrypted messaging, given that extremists tend to use encrypted platforms and virtual private networks to protect their messages and disguise their location.

Under the Terrorism Act 2000, the Home Secretary can proscribe an organisation if it is believed to have committed, planned or encouraged terrorist acts.

In June 2021, a Somerset man was jailed for 23 years for sharing terrorist material and possession of explosives.

Dean Morrice, 34, was found to have extreme right-wing material at his home, including manuals about how to make guns and guerrilla warfare.

Counter terrorism officers also found a 3D printer at his home along with evidence he was trying to make a weapon.

A Government spokeswoman added: 'The Government takes the threat from all forms of terrorism seriously, including the warped ideology of the extreme right-wing. We are committed to tackling those who spread views that promote violence and hatred against individuals and communities in our society, and that radicalise others.

'Our world class counter terrorism system is effective at identifying and disrupting extreme right-wing terrorist groups. Proscription plays a vital role, making it an offence to be a member or supporter of these groups, and sends a clear message that these vile ideologies have no place in society.'

Parliament's Intelligence and Security Committee has also raised concerns over the rise in right-wing extremists.

The committee's annual report, which was published earlier this month, found that 'the number of extreme right-wing terrorism investigations, disruptions and Prevent referrals have all increased steadily since 2017'.

The report said that the perpetrators of lone actor attacks 'often display an interest in military culture, weaponry and the armed forces or law enforcement organisations', and pointed to risks from both former and serving personnel.

The committee, chaired by Conservative MP Julian Lewis, added: 'The fact that the armed forces do not provide clear direction to service personnel regarding the membership of any organisation, let alone an extremist one, would therefore appear to be something of an anomaly.

'It appears a somewhat risky approach, given the sensitive roles of many service personnel.'

28 December 2022

The above information is reprinted with kind permission from *i* News.
© 2023 Associated Newspapers Limited

www.inews.co.uk

Extremism in the UK: new definitions threaten human and civil rights

An article from The Conversation.

By Chris Allen, Associate Professor, School of Criminology, University of Leicester

The UK government's approach to dealing with extremism has been enormously controversial since its strategy designed to counter it was released in 2015.

After years of invoking the subjective idea that extremists oppose 'fundamental British values', the government's current definition of extremism has been decried as unfit for purpose, with some far right-wing groups even using it to their advantage.

The UK government currently defines extremism as, 'vocal or active opposition to fundamental British values, including democracy, the rule of law, individual liberty and mutual respect and tolerance of different faiths and beliefs'. But this definition and its emphasis on 'fundamental British values' allows the far right to lean further into nationalism and distance themselves from allegations of extremism.

Research has also shown that the definition reinforces Islamophobic tropes while drawing on the controversial positions on UK Muslim communities by previous governments. So, if the government's definition doesn't quite work, then what exactly will?

In recent weeks, two new interventions have attempted to address the problem. The first is a report from the Commission for Countering Extremism. The second comes in the form of proposals from Her Majesty's Inspectorate of Constabulary and Fire and Rescue Services. Sadly, neither offer better ways of understanding how to define or to effectively respond to extremism. There's even potential for one to contradict the other.

Before we can come up with more suitable alternatives, it's worth wrapping our heads around these two approaches.

A new definition

The Commission for Countering Extremism has been critical of the government's definition and its shortfalls. While it's correct to point out these flaws, the commission's own explanation of 'hateful extremism' is also concerning. Under the commission's definition, hateful extremism includes behaviours which:

- Incite and amplify hate, engage in persistent hatred, or equivocate about and make the moral case for violence
- Draw on hateful, hostile or supremacist beliefs directed at groups perceived as threats to the well-being, survival or success of another group
- And cause (or are likely to cause) harm to individuals, communities or wider society

Much of this is open to interpretation, which means the definition could be applied inconsistently. It could also be unfairly applied to people or organisations that the

> **Key Fact**
> - The UK Government currently defines extremism as, 'vocal or active opposition to fundamental British values, including democracy, the rule of law, individual liberty and mutual respect and tolerance of different faiths and beliefs'.

government disagrees with. And that's without addressing the fact that many of these offending behaviours are already covered by existing legislation. The incitement of racial or religious hatred is addressed under the Racial and Religious Hatred Act 2006, the glorification of terrorist violence under the Terrorism Act 2006, and offences perceived to be motivated by hostility or prejudice are covered by the Crime and Disorder Act 1998 and Criminal Justice Act 2003.

The fact that the commission now wants hateful extremism to be seen as akin to hate crime is also a cause for concern. Actions it considers examples of 'hateful extremism' include:

- Disseminating extremist propaganda and disinformation
- Radicalising, indoctrinating and recruiting others to extremist ideologies
- Inciting, inspiring, encouraging, glorifying or justifying violence against certain outgroups (groups those involved don't identify with)

These criteria have the potential to be used against innocent, or non-violent ideological or political views. Salman Rushdie's book *The Satanic Verses*, which faced calls to be banned by all over the world in the late 1980s, could have easily been classified as an example of 'hateful extremism' at the time because of perceptions that it was inherently Islamophobic.

Questionable positions promoted by the far right could also carry more weight. Calls from the likes of Dutch politician Geert Wilders to ban the Qur'an in 2017, for example, could easily be parroted under the commission's understanding of 'hateful extremism'. But arguably, Wilders' rhetoric could be seen as inciting and amplifying hate, drawing on hateful, hostile or supremacist beliefs directed at Muslims and causing potential harm to those individuals, communities or wider society.

Turning away from 'domestic extremism'

The Inspectorate of Constabulary and Fire and Rescue Services' intervention focuses on changing terminology and no longer using 'domestic extremism', which had long been subject to criticism for its vagueness.

As David Anderson, the UK's independent reviewer of terrorism legislation, said in 2017, domestic extremism was:

> 'An amorphous concept, stretching from groups which currently pose no more than occasional public order concerns (animal rights, anti-fracking) to attack-planning by associates of the proscribed XRW (extreme right-wing) terrorist organisation National Action.'

The network for police monitoring, Netpol, agrees, alleging that police forces had arbitrarily used the term to crack down on groups they appeared biased or hostile towards. Lists of domestic extremists issued by the police in the past have included non-violent groups like Animal Aid, Extinction Rebellion and the Vegan Society alongside extremely violent groups like Atomwaffen Division, National Action and Sonnenkreig Division. That the guidance was badged 'counter-terrorism policing' again highlights a worrying lack of distinction between extremism and terrorism.

Though the Inspectorate of Constabulary and Fire and Rescue Services' decision to abandon the term 'domestic extremism' is welcome, its intention to replace it with 'aggravated activist' is a problem. Because of this unclear wording, it's likely that non-violent groups that respect and observe human and civil rights will continue to be unfairly targeted, criminalising those who protest or hold views that go against social norms.

This, along with the recently introduced police, crime, sentencing and courts bill could also lead to more people potentially losing their right to protest. Among other things, the proposed legislation will give the police more extreme restrictions on public demonstrations.

It's not hard to imagine how movements for social progress we now celebrate would be targeted today. If say, the suffragettes had emerged a century later than they did, it's likely that under this criteria, they too would've been classed as 'extremists'.

We need a new response to extremism. A good start would be to revisit the government's confused strategy. Clearly laying out the differences between extremism and terrorism and how extremist views make people vulnerable to terrorism, if at all, is also necessary.

As the Commission and Inspectorate's interventions show, there also needs to be much more consistency in how extremism is understood and responded to across various bodies. Until that happens, relying on adjusting definitions alone will just prolong these issues.

29 March 2021

> **Consider**
> What is the difference between terrorism and extremism?

THE CONVERSATION
The above information is reprinted with kind permission from The Conversation.
© 2010-2023, The Conversation Trust (UK) Limited

www.theconversation.com

'I mean you no harm': from troubled teen to neo-Nazi foot soldier

How a global white supremacist movement is recruiting American teenagers.

By Bryan Bender, Alexander Nabert and Christina Brause

LAS VEGAS, Nevada – When Conor Climo was winning plaudits for his sharp intellect in Arbor View High School's class of 2014, no one imagined he would soon be storing bomb-making material in his bedroom closet in preparation for a race war in the name of Adolf Hitler.

'He knew every element in the periodic table,' recalled classmate Lexi Epley.

Climo was a friendly, smart kid but as he grew into a lanky teen with a military-style haircut he became increasingly isolated, angry and – to some classmates – unstable.

'He was exiled a lot,' said Ebony Humes, who first became friendly with him in 6th grade. 'He would try to make friends, but people most of the time would turn their backs, or act as if he wasn't there. It kind of broke my heart. He did try, consistently, for years. You could see, in his face, the hurt.'

'He was a sweet kid,' echoed Epley. 'But people weren't very nice to him. He was bullied a lot.'

By 11th grade, Climo was nearly boiling over with resentment. 'No one likes me. I hate it here,' he sobbed in the cafeteria, at one point banging on the table, Humes recalled. 'I want out.'

It was after graduation that Climo, who lived with family at the end of a quiet cul-de-sac, found the community he lacked: a violent global movement hidden in the dark recesses of the internet bent on igniting a neo-Nazi race war, according to public documents, court records, law enforcement officials, and fellow classmates.

For more than a year, reporters from POLITICO, the German newspaper Welt and Insider uncovered the inner workings of this increasingly violent movement, drawn from nearly two dozen chat groups, more than 98,000 text and chat messages – including photos and videos – and interviews with members.

The data offers a rare peek into a burgeoning network of neo-Nazis threatening to kill politicians and journalists, providing instruction on how to build bombs and weapons with 3D printers, and encouraging each other to attack houses of worship, the gay community and people of colour. It's what extremism researchers call 'militant accelerationism' – a movement to spark a war for white power.

There are dozens of these groups on both sides of the Atlantic with martial names drawn from Nazi propaganda. Many followers have been influenced by the writings of James Mason, the 69-year-old Coloradan who joined an American Nazi party at age 14 and whose books and newsletter are considered modern-day Mein Kampfs for adherents.

Climo was drawn to The Feuerkrieg Division, which translates into 'fire war,' a moniker inspired by the torchlight marches at Nazi rallies in 1930s Germany.

FKD is believed to have been established in 2018 in Estonia and was thought to have quickly petered out. But there's been a resurgence in the last few years, according to law enforcement officials and experts in domestic extremist groups.

Involvement with the group led Climo to stockpile bomb-making materials in his bedroom. And as he increasingly embraced the cause of establishing a white ethno-state as his own, he was arrested after he was suspected of planning – and scouting out targets – to blow up a synagogue and gay bar, according to the FBI and court documents.

Climo pled guilty and was sentenced to two years on one count of possession of an unregistered firearm – specifically, the component parts of a destructive device.

Climo, who court records show was released earlier this year from federal prison and is now on three years' probation, did not respond to multiple requests for an interview. His family members also declined to speak on his behalf or did not respond to interview requests.

His journey from troubled American teen to neo-Nazi warrior was a wake up call and highlights the growing concerns about a new generation of virulent white supremacists emerging in America's suburbs or even in the ranks of the armed forces.

While Internet radicalisation has been recognized in recent years as a persistent threat – a handful of American teens have been charged with crimes related to online extremism – the international nature of the radicalisation has been far less appreciated.

By some estimates, FKD has just 100 members. But in an era where terrorism and mass violence is increasingly perpetrated by angry lone wolves, the group marks a dangerous evolution in a growing worldwide network of groups plotting in the shadows to enlist followers with military or firearms training to commit attacks on their own or in small groups.

'FKD is particularly alarming right now because it is so decentralized and really only present in online forums,' said Iris Malone, co-founder of the Mapping Militants Project and a consultant to the Department of Homeland Security. 'There is no one point of vulnerability where you can take them down. They will have multiple channels on Telegram or other online services where they can communicate with each other and they purposely build in redundant channels.'

In the United States, the FBI and other law enforcement have uncovered numerous ties to the online community in recent years, including a U.S. Army soldier who was sentenced to two years in prison for spreading information on social media about building a bomb and the chemical agent napalm.

It is a far more decentralized network compared to larger umbrella groups such as Atomwaffen, now known as the National Socialist Order. 'Atomwaffen, originally when it was formed, had members in Florida, or it had chapters in Washington,' Malone said. 'Having a physical organization or a physical address allows law enforcement authorities to go in and essentially be able to arrest or take down these groups.'

But what may be most troubling about the latest tendril is its heavy reliance on wayward teens.

'One of the main characteristics of the Feuerkrieg Division is the average age of the members, most of them being minors, starting from the age of 15,' concluded a 2021 study by the International Observatory on Terrorism Studies in Madrid, Spain.

The analysis also concluded that 'the terrorist group Feuerkrieg Division is recruiting again after being disbanded.'

Malone explained that online recruitment makes it especially challenging in the United States, where FKD is not designated a terrorist organization and authorities are faced with the often-competing demands of monitoring potentially dangerous online activities while not running afoul of civil liberties.

'I just don't think the government has a good handle on the online extremism stuff yet because of free speech issues and social media access,' she said.

'I mean you no harm'

Arbor View High School, in the Centennial Hills community of Las Vegas, looks like an ordinary suburban American public school campus in a diverse middle-class neighbourhood.

Near courtyard tables vandalized with sexually explicit graffiti, the main entrance is framed by a large mural quoting civil rights leader Dr. Martin Luther King, Jr.: 'The time is always right to do what is right.'

But while people of colour make up nearly half the student body, the school also has a history of racial tensions.

'There was diversity there but it was still very clear in some situations the separations and the tension between different cultural backgrounds,' recalled Humes, who is Black.

In 2019, two students were arrested and another cited after they targeted Black students with racist slurs on Instagram and threatened to attack them. One post read, 'God just seeing these n–ers [infuriates] me. I just wanna go Columbine...but only kill the f–king n–ers,' referring to the 1999 mass shooting in a Colorado high school.

Climo's own journey towards militancy broke out into the open in 2016, when he was working as a security guard.

A local news station featured him patrolling his neighbourhood wearing a flak jacket and carrying an AR-15 automatic rifle and four magazines – each containing 30 rounds of ammunition.

'I pretty much stay in constitutional bounds by doing this,' he said, insisting to a family of fleeing neighbours, 'I mean you no harm.'

'I remember thinking that's the last person who should have a gun in his hand,' recalled Humes, who now works for a local nonprofit that helps people with disabilities prepare to enter the job market.

A few months later, according to court documents, Climo was drawn to a question posed on a website called Quora: 'What are the downsides of multiculturalism?'

Climo, whose profile pic was a picture of an AR-15 rifle, answered by quoting Hitler. 'Your most precious possession on this Earth is your people!'

But over time he exhibited a desire to do something more than just post and provoke. 'I am more interested in action than online shit,' he later wrote in an online conversation, according to court records.

By then, according to the FBI, Climo was also using encrypted chat rooms like Discord that have come under increasing scrutiny for giving a platform to violent incitement where he regularly levelled anti-Semitic and racial slurs. And it was then he began discussing his violent plans with an FBI informant.

He detailed how to make a 'self contained molotov' explosive, according to the FBI. He boasted that he had been training to build an IED, or improvised explosive device. (Some of his fellow students later recalled he had started bragging about making bombs while still in high school.)

Climo privately shared with the FBI informant online that he was considering setting fire to a Las Vegas synagogue and that he tried unsuccessfully to recruit a homeless person to help him survey the building.

The FBI opened an investigation of Climo for 'communicating with individuals who identified with the white supremacist extremist group Attomwaffen Division,' according to the court documents, referring to the umbrella group that the Feuerkrieg Division grew out of.

FBI Special Agent Matthew James Schaeffer, a member of the Las vegas Joint Terrorism Task Force, described FKD in an affidavit as consisting mainly of white males between the ages of 16 and 30 'who all believe in the superiority of the white race.'

It pursues a 'leadership resistance' strategy that calls for followers, operating independently or in small groups, to challenge the established order and foment attacks on the federal government, minority communities, homosexuals, and Jews, he added.

In online conversations with an undercover agent, Climo also revealed scouting out other potential targets, including the Las Vegas office of the Anti-Defamation League, a prominent anti-hate organization, and a power plant that he referred to as a 'soft target,' according to court documents.

By the summer of 2019, the FBI reported in sworn testimony, he revealed he was scouting an area around a bar he said was frequented by homosexuals. He also shared screenshots of what he called a 'group of K--e synagogues locations in Vegas.' He proposed attacking one of them with a firearm and an explosive device, describing in detail how he would construct the bomb.

A court-ordered FBI search of his bedroom that August found multiple jars of bomb-making chemicals, wires, circuit boards, and his hand-drawn schematics. There were also a number of unregistered firearms, according to the federal indictment.

Climo recounted his activities for the FBI's Schaeffer, noting that he first communicated with the Feuerkrieg Division toward the end of 2017.

But upon his arrest, he told the FBI that he believed the group's goals were a 'righteous' cause.

'Jews suck,' he said.

New recruits

Climo's case is seen as a harbinger of what might lie ahead as the FBI, Department of Homeland Security and other law enforcement authorities pivot to what they see as one of the biggest domestic terror threats.

'Individuals subscribing to violent ideologies such as violent white supremacy, which are grounded in racial, ethnic, and religious hatred and the dehumanizing of portions of the American community, as well as violent anti–government ideologies, are responsible for a substantial portion of today's domestic terrorism,' states the White House's latest National Strategy for Countering Domestic Terrorism.

Increasingly, that also means isolated youngsters who spend lots of time alone and on the Internet.

The Anti-Defamation League recently reported that the Feuerkrieg Division is expanding its footprint across Europe – including Belgium, England, Ireland, the Netherlands, Norway, Latvia, Germany and Russia – as well as North America.

'In online chats, the group has actively sought out new recruits in Texas, the Great Lakes region, California, the Midwest, New Jersey, New York, and Philadelphia,' it found.

One FKD appeal on 8chan, an online message board that bills itself as a home for free speech but is also known to be a safe haven for far-right extremists, reads: 'Train and prepare for the collapse and meet up with fellow national socialist comrades.'

The online nature 'has important counterterrorism implications because it means that if the government just bans the organization, that's practically meaningless,' stressed Malone. 'It is not a physical organization like Al Qaeda was.'

Also fuelling the recruitment efforts, she fears, are recent racially motivated mass shootings, including in El Paso, Texas, and Buffalo, New York, which create 'a common set of martyr myths.'

But spotting these domestic terrorists in time may not be as easy as suggested by the case of Climo, whose brazen online communication was detected by law enforcement officials. Climo's federal public defender, Paul Riddle, said after his conviction that his client was grateful that he was nabbed before he went down a 'very dark path.'

'He's not on that path anymore, and he's not the same person that was arrested,' Riddle told the Las Vegas Sun.

But Humes said she ran into her longtime classmate just before he was arrested and asked him how he was doing.

She thought, 'Same old Conor, he still loves to talk.'

It was shocking, Humes said, to learn of the violent and racist turn he had taken. 'I saw him as the sweetheart that I remembered from high school and middle school.'

16 July 2022

Bender reported for POLITICO and Nabert and Brause for WELT AM SONNTAG. Nick Robins-Early of Insider contributed to this report.

The above information is reprinted with kind permission from POLITICO LLC.
© 2016 POLITICO LLC

www.politico.com

The Dover bombings were a hate attack – why did it take so long to call them terrorism?

Imagine a Muslim had committed a terrible act of violence – how long do you think it would be before they were labelled a terrorist?

By Nadeine Asbali, teacher and columnist

On October 30, Andrew Leak threw a number of incendiary devices at an immigration centre in Dover. The attack, which we can assume was against vulnerable and displaced people due to Leak's social media posts, was not initially treated as terrorism by police.

And yet, it took four days before the police publicly recognised that Leak's actions were acts of terrorism. It's taken even longer for many commenters on social media to see him as one.

When innocent Muslims are called 'terrorists' for doing nothing more than walking down the street due to the state of Islamophobia in this country, it's maddening that a genuine terrorist isn't given this label even when it's a fact.

November marks Islamophobia Awareness Month. A whole four weeks dedicated to the eradication of anti-Muslim prejudice and the awareness of how Islamophobia targets and decimates Muslim communities.

But Islamophobia is as rife as ever, awareness month or not. Here in Britain, we began the month with the Conservative Party scrapping plans to commit to a definition of Islamophobia and a terrorist attack perpetrated by an individual who declared he wanted to 'obliterate Muslim children' on social media.

Yet authorities were initially reluctant to call a spade a spade, and said his actions 'may not necessarily meet the threshold of terrorism', before later changing their minds.

Why is this? Is it because our anti-Muslim prejudices are so deep-rooted that on some level, we cannot conceive of a white man as a terrorist? Or ethnic minority, displaced people as victims of hate?

The horrific attack left two with minor injuries and culminated in Andrew Leak ending his own life. It solidifies the frightening reality that Islamophobic social media posts and dog-whistle racism aren't just empty words – they have real consequences.

And yet, in my opinion, the attack itself seems to have received far less coverage than other attacks, particularly those inspired by Islamist terrorism. Consider the difference in the coverage of the Parsons Green bombing in 2017 – enacted by someone with a Muslim name but who claimed to have been inspired by the Mission: Impossible films.

I have to ask, if Andrew had been a Muslim, would the media be interviewing his friends and conveniently including details about how, yes he shared far-right conspiracy theories about migrants on his Facebook but he was also friends with some people of colour (and therefore, not all that bad really)?

Would there be sympathetic quotes from neighbours about his health problems? When it was suggested that the Parsons Green bomber had been suffering from PTSD after arriving in the UK as teenage asylum seeker, I remember seeing disparaging posts all over social media mocking the

suggestion as a mere excuse, and even fuelling more anti-immigration rhetoric.

Would publications be pathologising his violence, trying to find some excuse for it buried in the mental health problems or financial difficulties of his past?

The short answer, in my opinion, is no.

Because deep down, as a nation, as a society, as a state, we still struggle to see a white man as a terrorist even if they are hurling bombs at innocent people. Because terrorists have brown skin and beards and shout 'Allahu Akbar'. Right?

In fact, Prevent counter-terrorism policy has been condemned previously for unfairly targeting Muslims. There have been claims of children being referred to Prevent for wearing a 'free Palestine' badge, another questioned for wearing a t-shirt with a slogan that teachers mistook for Isis propaganda, and one was reportedly questioned under the strategy for saying the word 'eco-terrorist'.

And yet, it appears that Andrew Leak's posts about obliterating Muslim children raised no flags. How did this man get away with it? If Prevent is also supposed to protect against right-wing terrorism too, how do men like Andrew slip through the net?

It has been reported that 41% of counter-terrorism arrests in 2021 were of suspects subscribing to far-right ideologies. In fact, in March of this year, the head of counter-terrorism, Matt Jukes, said that 19 out of 20 children who were arrested in the previous 12 months for terrorism offences were linked to an extreme rightwing ideology.

Why else did far-right atrocities such as the Finsbury Park Mosque attack in London not gain as much worldwide sympathy and attention as attacks fuelled by Islamist extremism?

This time, I've even more seen compassion shown towards Andrew Leak's motivations than I have for the individual victims of his attack and the conditions the government was holding them in.

Some people say that Islamophobia doesn't exist. Some say it's something made up by woke-obsessed Muslims intent on shutting down all criticism of our religion.

It's incredibly sad that something said 10 years ago by Baroness Warsi still holds true. She pointed out that Islamophobia was unique in that it 'passes the dinner table test'.

In other words, whip out a grotesquely Islamophobic trope at dinner, with colleagues or in the pub and nobody will shun you for your views, in fact they'll probably applaud them and package them in the language of immigration concern or countering extremism.

A decade later, Islamophobia has not gone anywhere – 42% of all hate crimes targeting religion were aimed at Muslims. It has morphed into something more potent, and even more embedded in the fabric of our society.

When we have a Home Secretary who describes the arrival of displaced people to the shores of Britain as an 'invasion' – many of whom hail from Muslim countries such as Afghanistan and Syria – what message does that send?

When she boasts that her 'dream' is to see a plane take off to Rwanda – a policy that the government's own review admitted has a greater impact on Muslim asylum seekers – that is Islamophobia in action, at the very heart of government and its policies.

We are witnessing first-hand a resurgence of the mentality that has always seen Muslims as invaders, and Islam as something that tarnishes superior western lands. The 'us versus them' agenda being peddled by the far-right, by politicians and by the press is an extension of that.

It suits the government and its quotas and ideologies to view all asylum seekers as pernicious, pesky Muslims wanting to settle here and make all meat halal and the burka mandatory.

Because if the public believes that, then hard-right immigration policies become more palatable, such as those leaving thousands living in squalor in detention camps on British borders, or deporting people with perfectly legal claims to asylum and traumatic histories halfway across the world.

Islamophobia is not political correctness gone mad and it is not just being called a 'terrorist' in the street or refused a job unless you remove your hijab. It is the creation of a hostile and dangerous environment in which Muslims are acceptable and worthy victims of discrimination, detention and even violence.

The attack in Dover only cements this. Islamophobia is the environment that allowed Andrew Leak to repeatedly post anti-Muslim hate. It is the environment that allowed the government to keep displaced people detained in such inhumane circumstances.

It is the environment that allowed the Home Secretary to refer to those seeking asylum as 'invading'. And it is the environment that allowed bombs to be thrown indiscriminately on innocent people because of where they came from and who they are.

10 November 2022

Key Facts

- It has been reported that 41% of counter-terrorism arrests in 2021 were of suspects subscribing to far-right ideologies.
- 42% of all hate crimes targeting religion were aimed at Muslims.

The above information is reprinted with kind permission from *Metro*.
© 2023 Associated Newspapers Ltd

www.metro.co.uk

Chapter 2

Tackling Terrorism

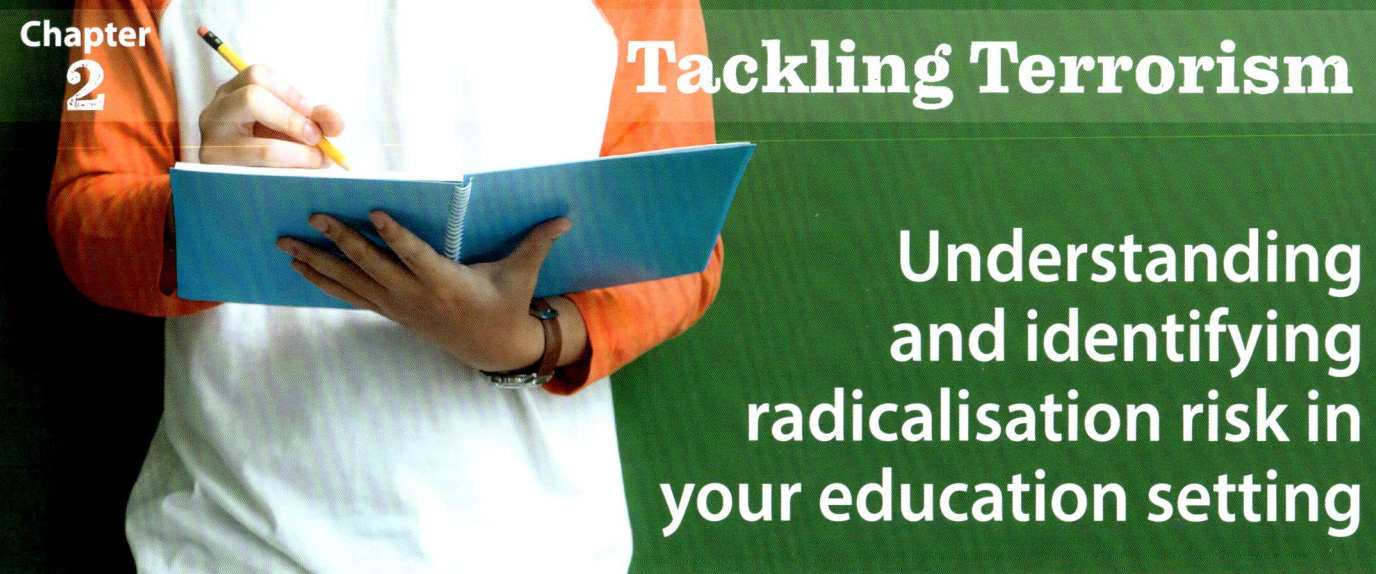

Understanding and identifying radicalisation risk in your education setting

To safeguard children, young people and adult learners who are vulnerable to radicalisation, designated safeguarding leads (DSLs) will need to take a risk-based approach.

The DSL should understand the risk of radicalisation in their area and educational setting. This risk will vary greatly and can change quickly, but nowhere is risk free.

To understand the risks or threats in your area, contact your:

- Prevent coordinator or Prevent education officer in your local authority (if applicable)
- HEFE (higher education and further education) regional Prevent coordinator (if you have one)
- local policing team
- local authority or safeguarding children partnership
- local authority or police Prevent partners (for access to your counter-terrorism local profile)

The threat of terrorism

The Terrorism Act 2006 defines 'terrorism' as an action or threat designed to influence the government or intimidate the public. Its purpose is to advance a political, religious or ideological cause.

In summary, terrorism is an action that:

- endangers or causes serious violence to a person or people
- causes serious damage to property, or seriously interferes with or disrupts an electronic system
- is designed to influence the government or to intimidate the public

The Prevent duty provides a framework for specified authorities to respond to the changing nature of threat in the UK. The government's counter-terrorism (CONTEST) strategy 2018 says the main threat to the UK comes from Daesh or Al Qa'ida inspired terrorism, although extreme right-wing terrorism is a growing threat.

Some groups and organisations are proscribed. This means they're banned under counter-terrorism measures introduced under the Terrorism Act 2000 (for example, Daesh and National Action).

The Home Office has published a list of proscribed terrorist groups or organisations.

The extremism threat

The counter-terrorism (CONTEST) strategy 2018 defines 'extremism' as vocal or active opposition to the fundamental British values of:

- democracy
- the rule of law
- individual liberty
- mutual respect
- tolerance of people with different faiths and beliefs

Extremism also includes calls for the death of members of the armed forces, whether in this country or overseas. Some groups and organisations that promote extremist ideologies are not proscribed terrorist groups or organisations.

These groups support divisive or hateful narratives towards others, but may not promote extreme violence. For example, they may hold views that support the distrust or hatred of people with different faiths or undermine the principles of democracy.

Mixed, unclear or unstable cases

Some children, young people and adult learners may appear engaged with, or have adopted, a mixed, unclear or unstable ideology that supports extreme violence.

Mixed, unclear or unstable cases could include individuals who:

- show an interest in multiple extremist ideologies at the same time
- switch from one ideology to another over time
- target a 'perceived other' of some kind (perhaps based on gender or another protected characteristic), but do not otherwise identify with one particular terrorist ideology or cause - for example, involuntary celibates (incels) who direct their anger mainly at women
- are obsessed with massacre, or extreme or mass violence,

- without specifically targeting a particular group - for example, high school shootings
- may be vulnerable to being drawn into terrorism out of a sense of duty, or a desire for belonging, rather than out of any strongly held beliefs

Online radicalisation

Children, young people and adult learners are at risk of accessing inappropriate and harmful extremist content online. This could include downloading or sharing terrorist material, which could be a criminal act.

The internet and social media make spreading divisive and hateful narratives to millions of people easy. Extremist and terrorist groups and organisations use social media (for example, apps, forums, blogs, chat rooms) to identify and target vulnerable individuals.

You do not need to be an online expert to understand when a child, young person or adult learner is at risk of harm. You should deal with harmful online behaviour in the same way as offline activity.

Concerns that a child or young person is being radicalised online

Any child, young person or adult learner who uses the internet can be at risk of online abuse.

Education settings need to be aware of the risks and talk to children, young people and adult learners about staying safe online.

If you're concerned that a child, young person or adult learner is vulnerable to radicalisation online, you should follow your normal safeguarding procedures.

Radicalisation is like grooming. Whether this happens online or offline, you should treat it in the same way.

How children, young people and adult learners become vulnerable to radicalisation

There's no single way of identifying whether a child, young person or adult learner is likely to be susceptible to an extremist ideology or vulnerable to radicalisation.

The process of radicalisation is different for every individual. It can take place over a long period, or it can be very quick.

Children, young people and adult learners who are vulnerable to grooming for sexual exploitation, criminal exploitation or county lines, may also be vulnerable to radicalisation. Factors could include things like being a victim or witness of crime, abuse or bullying, or having personal or emotional difficulties.

Adverse childhood experiences, combined with specific influences from family and peers or online connections, may make someone more vulnerable to radicalisation.

Extremist influences could include, but are not limited to:

- family members having direct contact or involvement with extremist or terrorist groups
- staff members of an education or community setting promoting an extremist ideology
- peers promoting an extremist ideology or sharing extremist material
- access or exposure to online extremist material via social media or the internet - for example, propaganda including pictures, videos, blogs and fake news
- exposure to extremist, terrorist or other violent activity in overseas settings access or exposure to extremist leaflets, magazines or stickering
- exposure to extremist groups hosting marches, protests or stalls

Risk factors

Push and pull factors can make a child, young person or adult learner at risk of extremism or radicalisation. Often there are several risk factors present that, seen together, can cause concern.

Push factors

Push factors may include a child, young person or adult learner feeling:

- isolated
- they do not belong
- they have no purpose
- low self-esteem
- their aspirations are unmet
- anger or frustration
- a sense of injustice
- confused about life or the world
- real or perceived personal grievances

Pull factors

Pull factors could include an extremist or terrorist group, organisation or individual:

- offering a sense of community and a support network
- promising fulfilment or excitement
- making the child, young person or adult learner feel special and part of a wider mission
- offering a very narrow, manipulated version of an identity that often supports stereotypical gender norms
- offering inaccurate answers or falsehoods to grievances
- encouraging conspiracy theories
- promoting an 'us vs. them' mentality
- blaming specific communities for grievances
- encouraging the use of hatred and violent actions to get justice
- encouraging ideas of supremacy

24 October 2022

The above information is reprinted with kind permission from Department for Education
© Crown Copyright 2023
This information is licensed under the Open Government Licence v3.0
To view this licence, visit http://www.nationalarchives.gov.uk/doc/open-government-licence/

www.gov.uk

Ministers studying plans for UK child-specific terrorism orders

Official adviser recommends giving those arrested for low-level crimes a choice to accept help or face jail.

By Vikram Dodd, Police and crime correspondent

New legal terrorism orders specifically for children should be brought in to tackle the growing numbers being arrested, the official adviser on terrorism law has told the government.

Ministers are studying plans that would result in children being compelled to accept help or face jail, devised by Jonathan Hall KC, the independent reviewer of terrorism legislation.

The move comes as the number of children arrested has increased, mainly for lower-level terrorism offences, such as sharing propaganda or downloading material. The rise has been fuelled by growing internet use and an increase in terrorist propaganda available online, with children as young as 13 being arrested.

There are concerns that tackling such children with powerful terrorism laws stigmatises them when they are not yet fully mature. There is a growing belief among counter-terrorism officials that a section of those arrested, while clearly breaking terrorism laws, pose little threat of staging an attack.

Furthermore, their commitment to an ideological cause is not strong, with a substantial amount having mental health or other vulnerabilities that make them more susceptible to falling for terrorist propaganda.

The proposed new orders would carry legal force and, under them, children aged 17 or under who have been arrested for lower-level terrorism offences would be given a choice. They could either risk prosecution, imprisonment and a criminal record or accept stringent measures, Hall said.

Hall, whose role is to advise the government and parliament on terrorism laws, said: 'I'm not talking about the most serious cases, where prosecution will usually remain the best option. But during the last three years there has been a slew of internet cases where the suspected terrorist conduct all relates to what children are saying or downloading online.

'There is a repeat pattern of particular offences, which I call documentary offences – instruction manuals, terrorist publications, encouragement – all internet-based, where there is no evidence of attack-planning. These offences were created at a time when there was a clearer link between words and violence, in the context of the IRA and al-Qaida. That link is less clear for children online.'

Hall's proposals include monitoring software on their electronic devices to detect if they are accessing extremist material, limits on their use of devices, and potentially limits on whom they could contact. They would also have to attend mentoring sessions in an attempt to divert them from any belief in violent extremism.

> **Key Facts**
> - In the year to September 2020, 4% of those arrested were aged under 18.
> - In the year to September 2022, 17% of terrorism-related arrests were people under 18.
> - 32 arrests: 12 were suspected of extreme rightwing terrorism, 16 were suspected of Islamist extremism, and for four children the ideology could not be classified.

Under the plans being studied, breaching these conditions would in itself be an arrestable offence punishable by the courts. Complying with the conditions would avoid prosecution.

Figures from Counter Terrorism Policing show there has been a rapid growth of child terrorism suspects in England, Scotland and Wales.

In the year to September 2020, 4% of those arrested were aged under 18. But in the year to September 2022, 17% of terrorism-related arrests were people under 18. That equates to 32 arrests: 12 were suspected of extreme rightwing terrorism, 16 were suspected of Islamist extremism, and for four children the ideology could not be classified.

The effects of lockdown, with schools closed and children in their bedrooms and searching online, was also thought to be a factor.

Tim Jacques, the senior national coordinator for counter-terrorism, said: 'The increase in young people featuring in our casework is clear, perhaps demonstrated most starkly by the arrest statistics. We have often talked about how the terrorist threat is evolving, and consequently our response needs to evolve. Our role is to keep people safe from terrorism and we must consider all legitimate options to make this happen.'

Police have warned that children from middle-class backgrounds are being lured into extreme rightwing terrorism with online content based on violent video games shaped to indoctrinate them. Statistics for Prevent, the official deradicalisation scheme, also show a growing number of young people being referred.

A review of Prevent by the former Charity Commission chair, William Shawcross, has been completed and has been with the home secretary, Suella Braverman, since September. Its publication has been repeatedly delayed amid concerns parts of it may libel groups or individuals, and with departments across government still trying to reach agreement on a response to its findings and recommendations. It is expected to be published early in the new year.

Recent studies find that both those at risk of radicalisation but yet to offend and those convicted and in jail for terrorism offences have significant levels of mental health challenges or other vulnerabilities. Last year, the Guardian revealed that up to seven in 10 people referred to Prevent may experience mental ill health or other vulnerabilities that could leave them susceptible to falling for propaganda from violent extremists. Those involved in Prevent believe such psychological problems are much more of a potential factor than first thought.

Hall said the most serious cases involving children should still lead to prosecutions, and said police were right to arrest children for lower-level terrorism offences. 'Where there is a degree of uncertainty about the risk to the public, there will be no alternative to going through the door,' he said.

2 January 2023

The above information is reprinted with kind permission from *The Guardian*.
© 2023 Guardian News and Media Limited

www.theguardian.com

Hate preachers to be held in 'jails within jails' to stop radicalisation of fellow inmates

Review of Human Rights Act will make it easier to place terrorists in 'separation units' which nullify 'invidious influences'.

By Charles Hymas

More terrorists are to be held in 'jails within jails' to stop hate preachers influencing other prisoners.

Dominic Raab, the Justice Secretary, is preparing a major expansion of the use of 'separation centres' within high-security prisons where dangerous terrorists will be held for longer to keep them away from other vulnerable prisoners.

It will be supported by reforms to human rights laws designed to combat claims by the terrorists' lawyers that separating them from other prisoners breaches their rights to socialise.

There are three separation units in high-security jails in England and Wales, but they have been underused because of claims by lawyers that they breach prisoners' 'Article 8' rights to a family and private life.

In one case, convicted killer Jemmikai Orlebar-Forbes, 28, won £15,000 from the Government after claiming a breach of his Article 8 rights when he was segregated with other terror offenders at the high-security HMP Frankland in County Durham.

Signalling the move in the Commons on Tuesday, Mr Raab said: 'One of the challenges in dealing with terrorist offenders, particularly those who could infect the minds of others, is the issue of separation centres.

'We are increasingly seeing litigation claims, claiming the Article 8 right as a right to socialising, getting in our way. That's a good example of the common sense approach [to reform of the human rights laws] and the balance we want to have.'

Reforms proposed by Jonathan Hall, the independent reviewer of terrorism laws, are expected to be introduced to make it easier for prison governors to place terrorists in the centres at HMP Frankland, Full Sutton near York and Woodhill in Milton Keynes.

At present, there are just 10 terrorist prisoners held in the 'jails within jails', including Hashem Abedi who helped organise the Manchester Arena attack in which 23 people died.

It is understood the reforms will mean their placement in the centres will only be reviewed every two years, as opposed to the current three months, which means they could spend longer within them.

Decisions on whether a convicted terrorist is placed in a separation centre will be based on their level of risk rather than any single act they may have committed, which will make it easier to justify keeping them away from other inmates.

'Incapacitate the radicaliser'

Terrorists could also be placed within the units as soon as they enter the jail, after their trial, and on the basis of secret intelligence rather than solely on the basis of their offences.

'The Justice Secretary wants to streamline the process so that we can put people in [separation centres] much more easily and therefore protect the prison population from their invidious influences,' said a Government source.

'Additionally, if you reform the Human Rights Act, you can remove some of the obstacles that have stopped us putting them into these separation units.'

Ian Acheson, a former prison governor who reviewed extremism in jails for the Government, welcomed the moves. 'The policy benefits are clear for those few people in custody who, by their subversive behaviour, represent a threat to national security,' he said.

'You isolate people who are determined to continue proselytising hateful ideologies. You separate the hate preacher from their potential audience that they might radicalise. You break that relationship and incapacitate the radicaliser.

'You tell them they will stay there until you are satisfied that they no longer present a risk to national security and you have the opportunity to address that dangerous and risky behaviour.'

8 February 2022

The above information is reprinted with kind permission from *The Telegraph*.
© Telegraph Media Group Limited 2022

www.telegraph.co.uk

UN Security Council boosts commitment to fight digital terror

A two-day meeting of the UN Security Council Counter-Terrorism Committee in India has ended with the adoption of a document committing Member States to prevent and combat digital forms of terror, notably using drones, social media, and online terrorist financing.

The non-binding document, known as The Delhi Declaration on countering the use of new and emerging technologies for terrorist purposes, was adopted in the Indian capital on Saturday, following a series of panels that involved Member States representatives, UN officials, civil society entities, the private sector, and researchers.

The declaration aims to cover the main concerns surrounding the abuse of drones, information and communication technologies, new online payments and fundraising methods for terrorist purposes, and create guidelines that will help to tackle the growing issue.

'The Delhi declaration lays out the foundation for the way ahead,' said David Scharia from the Counter-Terrorism Executive Committee. 'It speaks about the importance of human rights, public-private partnership, civil society engagement, and how we are going to work together on this challenge. It also invites the CTED [the Secretariat for the Committee] to develop a set of guiding principles, which will result from intensive thinking with all the partners.'

Human rights at the core

Respect for human rights was highly stressed in the document, and during the debates. The UN Secretary-General, António Guterres, underscored that there must be 'concrete measures to reduce these vulnerabilities while committing to protect all human rights in the digital sphere.'

In a video message, Mr. Guterres added that human rights could only be achieved through effective multilateralism and international cooperation, with responses that are anchored in the values and obligations of the United Nations Charter and the Universal Declaration of Human Rights.

Representing the Human Rights Office, Scott Campbell, who leads the digital technology team, echoed the Secretary-General, explaining that 'respecting rights when countering terrorism is fundamental to ensuring sustainable and effective efforts to protect our security.'

'Approaches that cross these important lines not only violate the law, but they also undermine efforts to combat terrorism by eroding the trust, networks, and community that is essential to successful prevention and response,' he said.

Mr. Campbell argued that international law and human rights present many answers to the issue, recalling that the Member States have a duty to protect the security of their population and to ensure that their conduct does not violate the rights of any person.

Regulation and censorship

He also stressed that companies and States should be cautious when filtering and blocking social media content, as it can 'affect minorities and journalists in disproportionate ways.'

To overcome the issue, Mr. Campbell suggested that restrictions should be based on precise and narrowly tailored laws, and should not incentivize the censoring of legitimate expression. He argued that they should have transparent processes, genuinely independent and impartial oversight bodies, and that civil society and experts should be involved in developing, evaluating, and implementing regulations.

During the closing session of the meeting, the Committee chairperson, Ambassador Ruchira Kamboj of India, stated that the outcome document takes note of the challenges, and proposes 'practical, operational, and tactical possibilities of addressing the opportunities and the threats posed by the use of new and emerging technologies for terrorist purposes.'

She added that the global policymaking community 'must be agile, forward-thinking, and collaborative' to meet the changing needs of States facing new challenges from digital terror.

Delhi Declaration highlights:

- In the Delhi Declaration, Member States agree that guidelines and implemented actions should be based on international law and human rights.

- Members of the Committee will draft recommendations to counter the terrorist exploitation of Information and Communications Technology, payment technologies and fundraising methods and unmanned aerial systems (UAS, or drones).

- The body will assist Member States in the implementation of all relevant Security Council resolutions to countering the use of technologies for terrorist purposes, while respecting human rights and fundamental freedoms.

- A new set of non-binding guiding principles to assist Member States in countering the digital terrorism threat will be issued, with a compilation of good practices on the opportunities offered by the same set of technologies to tackle threats.

- The relevant offices will commit to deepening engagement and cooperation with civil society, including women and women's organizations, relevant private-sector entities, and other stakeholders, and build partnerships.

29 October 2022

From UN News, by Peace and Security, ©2023 United Nations.
Reprinted with the permission of the United Nations.

www.news.un.org

Where next in the fight against Islamist extremism?

By Will Baldet

- The answer must lie with moderate nations such as Jordan, Morocco and the UAE
- As Afghanistan shows only too well, Muslims suffer the most from a resurgence of Islamism
- There is now an 'arc of instability' from North Africa to South Asia

With Afghanistan and the 9/11 anniversary dominating recent news, and early indications of al-Qaeda regrouping, attention has understandably settled once again on the Islamist ideology that still represents such a menace to our way of life. Indeed, Tony Blair recently warned that Islamism remains a 'first-order security threat to the West'.

Those of us who work in counter-terrorism unequivocally separate the politics of Islamism from the religion of Islam, but the role of ideology in a person's radicalisation continues to divide experts.

Some argue that ideology has lost its relevance. Instead, they see radicalisation as representative of a steady move in society towards legitimising violence in pursuit of utopian ideals. This argument has some merit. If a society fails to fulfil people's expectations, then perhaps civil unrest and violence gain legitimacy for those impatient with the current system. Terrorists themselves have justified their actions in these terms, but such frustrations are common the world over and almost no one would contemplate murdering children at a concert or detonating a bomb on a crowded train.

Other experts say ideology remains paramount. They point to the tens of thousands of ISIS recruits who travelled to a warzone to join an organisation committed to brutal, theocratic totalitarianism. Similarly, extreme right-wing accelerationism attracts a large online following, despite its commitment to white supremacy and destabilising society through rape, paedophilia and murder.

The truth lies somewhere between these two points of view. For many would-be extremists there will be underlying grievances that increase susceptibility to radicalisation, but ideology is the driving force that gives them purpose. Similarly, the lives of terrorists are often littered with social

and psychological fractures that make extremist narratives a compelling way to make sense of life's injustices. Whatever their individual trajectories, ideology gives a twisted moral clarity to their cause and while extreme right-wing violence is on the rise, Islamist terrorism remains the UK's leading threat, as it has done since Bin Laden's fatwa against the West.

Much of al-Qaeda's terrorism was planned from within Taliban-controlled Afghanistan, which harboured the terrorists and their training camps. Given their record, we are right to be asking what the Taliban takeover of Afghanistan means for global terror. This quote by Maulawi Hafiz Mohibullah Muktaz, a religious leader and fighter from Kandahar, offers no reassurance:

'....here is proof of the power of faith and God and jihad. On the back of victory, I hope we can use Bagram as a place to spread jihad further into the region and Muslim world.'

We typically view the Islamist threat through a Western lens: what does it mean for us, when is the next attack and how can we resist the increasingly confident Islamist advances of ISIS, al-Qaeda, al-Shabaab and other terrorist organisations?

This is an understandable but overly narrow perspective. As is often pointed out, far more Muslims are killed in terror attacks than non-Muslims, and Islamic countries will be the first to suffer from any campaign to 'spread jihad further into the region'. That means we should join-up our thinking with non-Western partners to collectively consign Islamist extremism to the margins. The answer must lie with moderate nations such as Jordan, Morocco and the UAE who reject Islamism's attempts to consume Islam.

There are encouraging examples too. A few years ago, for instance, a Jordanian colleague told me how he protected his youth centres from the grip of Abu Musab al-Zarqawi, who went on to become leader of al-Qaeda in Iraq. Former al-Qaeda propagandist Jessie Morton has spoken of his 'deradicalisation' in Morocco, facilitated by an environment in which Muslims embraced their faith as a religion and not a political ideology.

As Anne-Elisabeth Moutet noted in a recent CapX piece, the UAE's fight against political Islam – in particular the Muslim Brotherhood – is arguably the highest-profile in the Muslim world. It proactively seeks to reject Islamism by projecting an image of a tolerant nation willing to reach out to secular allies, including Israel. Abu Dhabi also plays host to the Hedayah Centre, a world-leading organisation equipping people with the tools to counter extremist narratives.

Where, then, is the renewed Islamist threat emanating from?

Ali Soufan, a former FBI Special Agent and author of *The Black Banners: The Inside Story of 9/11 and the War Against Al-Qaeda*, refers to an 'arc of instability' from North Africa to South Asia, with significant territory in Libya, Somalia, Yemen, Syria, Lebanon and Iraq governed by non-state Islamist militias. All of these groups share a deep hatred of the West and its allies, and many have fallen under the influence of the Iranian regime.

The newly announced AUSUK pact shows that Western powers are still capable of acting in concert to tackle specific threats. But tackling terrorism is not just about hard power – we cannot hope to defeat extremism without tackling the ideologies that lie behind it. The 20 years since 9/11 have taught us that Western apathy and timidity only emboldens Islamism. If we cannot marshal the political courage to reject this cynical ideology, working with Muslim partners in the Middle East, the next 20 years could be every bit as difficult as the last two decades.

20 September 2021

The above information is reprinted with kind permission from CAPX
© CENTRE FOR POLICY STUDIES 2023

www.capx.co

Terrorist recruitment now happens mainly online – which makes offenders easier to catch

An article from The Conversation.

By Jens Binder, Senior Lecturer in Psychology, Nottingham Trent University and Chris Baker-Beall, Senior Lecturer in Crisis and Disaster Management, Bournemouth University.

It is notoriously difficult to work out how and why someone becomes a terrorism risk. While attacks cause immense pain and suffering, the actual number of terrorist incidents in the western world is small. That makes it difficult to arrive at reliable, quantified evidence.

But in our research, we've started to identify important patterns when it comes to different journeys into extremist offending. Most notably, we've found that in recent years, people who go on to be convicted of terrorist offences are far more likely to have been radicalised online – without any offline interactions at all – than was the case in the past.

While the seeming ease with which this can happen is worrying, we've also found that people recruited purely online are less likely to commit violent attacks and less committed to their extremist causes than those recruited via in-person meetings. While face-to-face radicalisation continues, the process is now found to take place primarily online.

Our work, which uses detailed risk assessment reports on people sentenced for terrorist offences in England and Wales, draws on 437 cases between October 2010 and December 2021. These reports, written by trained prison and probation professionals, focus on the pre-history of an offence and the current circumstances of the offender. As well as a detailed narrative, they also contain estimates of the levels of risk that the individual poses.

The shift online

We wanted to look into how people became radicalised in the outside world before they committed an extremist offence. We found that, over time, it is less and less the case that people are radicalised offline, such as at local meeting places or via direct contact with peers and relatives.

Mixed radicalisation, where extremist offenders are subject to both online and in-person influences, has also been declining. It is now much more common for people to be radicalised online. They might learn from online sources or engage with extreme views on social media. They might also use internet forums and chat groups that provide easy access to like-minded others.

Our findings show that despite current perceptions about the growth of encrypted messaging services, online radicalisation is not necessarily happening predominantly through one-to-one communication channels. The most commonly named platform is YouTube.

While encrypted applications will always play their role, monitoring and regulating the more public online spaces is likely to make the most difference.

It was also interesting to note that those radicalised online consistently showed the lowest level of estimated risk. They were less engaged with extremist causes than those radicalised offline. They were also the most likely to have committed a non-violent offence, such as inciting and encouraging others to commit terrorism or possessing terrorist material, and to have committed their offences solely online.

They were also far less intent on committing further offences after leaving prison than those who were radicalised offline – and they appeared to have the lowest capacity to commit further crimes because of having less access to the knowledge, networks or materials they might need.

So it seems that while online radicalisation is the most pervasive form at the moment, it is not overly effective at permanently immersing people in an extremist mindset. Nor is the online approach particularly successful for conveying the skills and knowledge necessary to commit graver offences.

Disrupting online plots

In order to check for potentially more dangerous sub-groups, we also focused on those offenders classed as attackers. These were people who did not necessarily carry out full attacks but had, at the very least, cast themselves in such a role and had pursued attack plans.

The online group showed the lowest frequency of attack-related activities, and attackers in this group were least successful in progressing plots for attacks. Only 29% of these plots moved from planning to the execution stage and only 18% were successfully carried out.

All the plots we studied, which were not successful, had been disrupted by the police or other security services. The online world is, after all, not a perfect hiding place. Online activities often leave traces that can be detected by counter-terrorism practitioners.

While this could all mean that online radicalisation is comparatively harmless, there is a thin line between a relatively ineffective online-only radicalisation and a much more effective mixed radicalisation that includes both online and in-person influences. Online communication can slide into real-life interactions, and people radicalised via the latter technique were assessed as being highest in engagement and intent.

So while the switch to online radicalisation appears to make people easier to catch and less likely to commit violent attacks, this form of radicalisation should still be taken seriously and be recognised as a potential stepping stone towards more dangerous behaviour.

22 December 2022

The above information is reprinted with kind permission from The Conversation.

© 2010-2023, The Conversation Trust (UK) Limited

www.theconversation.com

Why dialogue is an essential tool for peace, security and development

The hatred and ignorance that breed violent extremism thrives when we stop talking. Intercultural dialogues could be a viable solution.

By Gabriela Ramos, Assistant Director-General for the Social and Human Sciences, United Nations Educational, Scientific and Cultural Organization (UNESCO)

- Violent extremism is rising globally, with a 17% increase in attacks recorded in 2021.
- Somalia and Kenya are two countries that have experienced significant impacts of Al Shabaab's violence and the group has been linked to 22,000 fatalities since 2008.
- Intercultural dialogue can open up channels of communication and foster understanding between groups from different cultures.

Violent extremism is born from distorted interpretations of culture, hatred and ignorance and threatens our societies' foundations – tearing us apart and weakening collaboration. And according to the Global Peace Index 2022, violent extremism is on the rise, with a 17% increase in attacks in 2021.

East Africa is a region where violent extremism is particularly rife, with Al-Shabaab – rooted initially in Somalia – having spread their campaign of terror to neighbouring Ethiopia, Kenya and Uganda. The group has been involved in more than 8,400 events linked to more than 22,000 fatalities since 2008. Though there has been a 17% decline in terrorism deaths attributed to the group, they still ranked among the four deadliest terrorist outfits in the world in 2021.

Somalia and Kenya have had to live in the shadow of terrorism for far too long. Somalia is the third most impacted country by terrorism for the fifth consecutive year, according to the Global Terrorism Index 2022. In 2021 alone, 599 people died and 479 were injured due to 308 terrorist incidents in Somalia. In recent years the intensity of the Al-Shabaab threat in Kenya has declined, yet the memory of the attacks on the Westgate Mall in 2013 and Garissa University in 2015 looms large to this day.

Therefore, the question remains: What can be done to address this hatred and ignorance which rips societies apart? How can it be stopped?

To counter violent extremism, we need to talk

Intercultural dialogue occurs when different groups commit to engaging in meaningful, open communication that creates connections and breaks down barriers. An important tool for peace, security and development, intercultural dialogue has been used throughout the world to combat hatred and ignorance.

In Kenya, intercultural dialogue is countering violent extremism and promoting sustainable peace and human rights. In 2019, the Inter-Religious Council of Kenya (ICRK) launched 'Building Intercultural Bridges,' which turns to intercultural dialogue to foster contact and understanding between Christian and Muslim communities and supports youth who experience exclusion, lack of opportunities and vulnerability to recruitment by violent extremist groups.

In an interview for the ICRK, Ali Amani Babu, a youth from Mombasa who participated in the programme, attested, 'We had been made to believe that these two religions are sworn enemies and they can't tolerate each other. Through this programme, we were able to change that perception and now we are able to cooperate in all activities in our communities.'

Recognizing the potential of intercultural dialogue and the growing need for tools that support collaboration, UNESCO launched the Initiative for Enabling Intercultural Dialogue in partnership with the Institute for Economics and Peace. The partnership has just launched a report containing data proving the efficacy of intercultural dialogue in improving social cohesion and social inclusion for the first time. The report draws on data from 160 countries in all world regions.

Intercultural dialogues: a solution for peace

'Through this programme ... we are now we are able to cooperate in all activities in our communities.'

– Ali Amani Babu, Participant in Building Intercultural Bridges, Mombasa

Findings highlighted in the UNESCO report launched under this initiative – We Need To Talk – show that intercultural dialogue can make a real difference. Between 2015 and 2019, 69% of terrorist attacks and 89% of deaths from terrorism globally occurred in countries where dialogue between opposing groups is stalling. Conversely, countries with higher dialogue levels see higher peacefulness and human rights protection. Programmes based on intercultural dialogue, like Building Intercultural Bridges, offer spaces to learn about 'others' and ultimately break down existing barriers and promote understanding.

Policies and actions that enable intercultural dialogue can have widespread impacts. UNESCO's new framework offers communities a guide on how to maximize impact for the first time. We will see transformation in our world if we take advantage of this important new data.

When we stop talking, solutions to tensions and conflict become impossible. The hatred and ignorance that breed violent extremism thrives when we stop talking. There is not one easy solution to addressing groups such as Al-Shabaab and their impacts but intercultural dialogue can be leveraged to forge divides and bring communities together again. Let us allow UNESCO's new framework to guide us to a better tomorrow.

3 October 2022

The views expressed in this article are those of the author alone and not the World Economic Forum.

Key Facts

- According to the Global Peace Index 2022, violent extremism is on the rise, with a 17% increase in attacks in 2021.
- Al-Shabaab has been involved in more than 8,400 events linked to more than 22,000 fatalities since 2008.
- Between 2015 and 2019, 69% of terrorist attacks and 89% of deaths from terrorism globally occurred in countries where dialogue between opposing groups is stalling.

Write

Write a couple of paragraphs describing peace processes. Can you give some examples of successful peace processes that have ended terrorist activities either domestically or globally?

The above information is reprinted with kind permission from World Economic Forum
© 2023 World Economic Forum

www.weforum.org

Should we forgive extremists?

Peter Cytanovic is used to being hated.

By Charlotte McDonald-Gibson

Peter Cytanovic has become so accustomed to being hated that he rattles off some of the shocking messages he has received with the ease of going through a shopping list: 'Why don't you just kill yourself?'; 'I'm going to come to Reno and kill you'; 'Die Nazi scum.'

Nearly five years ago, on August 11, 2017, Cytanovic travelled to Charlottesville, Virginia, to attend the Unite the Right rally, a gathering of white nationalists including Klu Klux Klan members, neo-Nazis, and white supremacists. As night fell, the angry crowd marched and chanted racist and anti-Semitic slogans. Cytanovic was in the thick of it, holding a tiki-torch aloft as he screamed at counter-protesters. A photographer captured the moment. Soon, his picture was everywhere. 'I was the face of white terror,' he tells me.

At the time, Cytanovic identified as a white nationalist, and held racist views: he supported the deportation of migrants and the creation of a white-only state. By the time I met him, in the summer of 2019, he had recanted. He was nearing the end of a Masters in Political Theory at the London School of Economics, volunteering with a counter-extremism organisation, and optimistic about how he could use his experiences to help others understand – and avoid – the draw of the extreme Right.

But his story raises difficult questions about how far a person must go to make amends, and whether efforts to silence people like him – however well-intentioned those efforts might be – help or hinder the battle to combat polarisation and extremism.

Cytanovic's journey to radicalisation follows a familiar path at first. He was born into a working-class family in Reno, Nevada, in 1996. His mother was diagnosed with brain cancer while pregnant with him, and the cost of the treatment would leave the family crippled by a lifetime of debt. His father lost his job as a bookie when a foreign company bought the casino where he worked. Still, Cytanovic graduated from high school with good grades and began studying politics at the University of Nevada.

It was a difficult transition. Cytanovic says he felt a gulf between himself and the generally richer students, particularly as his conservative Catholic views clashed with those of his more socially liberal peers. During his early years at college, he felt dismissed as 'white trash', although he also admits that he often acted like 'a genuine asshole'.

He was drawn to Donald Trump because he seemed to understand the frustrations of poor white communities. Then he began to spend increasing amounts of time watching alt-Right content on YouTube – 'trying to find myself' – and soon found himself down rabbit holes of his own biases, now amplified and distorted by the social media algorithms that were offering up ever more extreme-Right content.

Cytanovic eventually joined Identity Evropa, which the Southern Poverty Law Center says was, at the time, 'at the forefront of the racist 'alt-right's' effort to recruit white, college-aged men and transform them into the fashionable new face of white nationalism'. They were one of the organisers of the Unite the Right rally in Charlottesville, and while Cytanovic says he was never anti-Semitic, he was fully aware of the presence of neo-Nazis at the march.

I have quizzed Cytanovic at length about what he believed when he attended the rally and how his views have changed (he has since apologised for his actions and worked with organisations countering hate to try to make amends). I have also spoken to counter-extremism and de-radicalisation experts who have worked alongside him over the past five years. I am confident that he is not a neo-Nazi or a white nationalist.

But that doesn't mean his transformation has been total. In the immediate aftermath of the rally, Cytanovic was unrepentant, giving interviews about his white nationalist beliefs. The first seeds of doubt were sown when he befriended a young Muslim-American woman affiliated with the Democrat Party: she challenged his views without insulting him, allowing him to understand the hurt he had caused.

'I give her the most credit for being the most patient, for really allowing me to calm down, to loosen up, to realise that I didn't need to be so defensive and start to really think about everything,' he says. 'I don't think there was a day when I suddenly said, I want to make amends. It developed over time as I realised how wrong I was.'

Still, his expressions of regret are often countered by self-justifications; he can swing from showing genuine awareness that his past views were racist, to defensive outbursts on issues like migration. He gets agitated when he feels like his socially conservative beliefs are under attack, or when they are equated with the views of the neo-Nazis. An interview with LSE's student newspaper in Spring 2019, in which he wanted to apologise for attending the Charlottesville rally, backfired when he made derogatory remarks about trans people while trying to explain his Catholic beliefs.

If we are serious about countering radicalisation, though, we do need to pay attention to people like Cytanovic, because his messy and complicated retreat from the extreme reflects the reality of increasing numbers of people across the world. It also poses difficult questions about the consequences far-Right extremists should face. Soon after Charlottesville, the FBI questioned Cytanovic and decided to take no action against him; his judgement lies in the hands of society.

When studying in London he felt like a chance of redemption was within his grasp. He volunteered at Groundswell, a community organisation aimed at countering extremism by building bridges between different groups. But since he returned to Reno, later in 2019, Cytanovic has been struggling to see a future for himself.

He has been unable to find a job outside factory work. When he does find work, he is routinely fired when his past is unearthed. No university will accept him for further study. Even efforts to volunteer at community or religious organisations are turned down. Institutions and groups are, understandably, reluctant to associate with him.

Meanwhile, as well as receiving death threats, he is still insulted on the street, and bombarded with hate mail. When he tried to join the National Guard, media reports framed it as an attempt by the far-Right to infiltrate the military. All of which leaves him in a Catch-22 situation: 'No one ever believes I have good intentions. I'm a Nazi until proven otherwise, but I can't get the opportunity to prove I'm not.'

Who cares? That's the question people often ask when I talk to them about Cytanovic, who is one of eight former extremists featured in my book *Far Out: Encounters with Extremists*. Why should anyone care that a man who openly and knowingly marched alongside the KKK is struggling to build a normal life?

It's an important question to ask. In the aftermath of Trump's election, there was a shift in media coverage: many outlets profiled Americans with white nationalist ideologies in an effort to understand the mainstreaming of racist beliefs. But such stories often missed the mark, portraying the 'neo-Nazi next door' without offering much insight into the hugely complex radicalisation process. And some unwittingly caused harm by giving a platform to extremist views.

Now there has been a swing in the other direction, illustrated by a headline a few years ago: 'We Need to Stop Humanising Neo-Nazis'. Attempts to explore the human motives for extremism are now often considered taboo. Coverage is expected to be outright condemnatory, rather than focused on the potential for rehabilitation.

Since meeting Cytanovic, I have tried to publish articles about him at points when his story seemed relevant – with the election of Joe Biden, for example, when the US might have been seeking solutions to a large radicalised population. Publications would initially be enthusiastic, before deciding not to pursue the story. Reasons given included that Cytanovic was undeserving of any media coverage.

The focus has shifted now from victims of extremism – which, in many ways, is a good thing. But we're in danger of oversimplifying the perpetrators. When it comes to their stories, the world wants black-and-white tales of complete U-turns, even when they misunderstand the complexities of de-radicalisation or raise questions about their authenticity. Two organisers of the Charlottesville rally, for example, claimed to have reformed and started a counter-extremism group. Their apparently miraculous conversions earned much media coverage, despite accusations that they were just trying to clean up their images as they faced lawsuits over the Charlottesville violence.

Cytanovic's attempts at honesty seem to be his undoing. While at times his motives can veer towards self-serving – like most people's – it is also clear that he has interrogated his past beliefs and is genuinely seeking to help others, while remaining authentic to his religious framework. And if people are serious about countering extremism, it's important to understand the nuance of de-radicalisation. Cytanovic's frankness offers an important insight into that process – and provides clues for those planning interventions that can bring people back from the brink.

That's why we need to have the courage to explore difficult and controversial aspects of de-radicalisation in the media – and understand that while these stories will never be simple, they cannot simply be erased.

By eternally excluding him, society runs a risk. Feelings of alienation and isolation can help drive people to extreme groups, so marginalising anyone attempting to reject those groups is likely to eventually backfire. It could lead people to return to hate groups, and enable re-radicalisation.

Right now, Cytanovic shows no sign of returning to the far-Right. He says he wants to make a positive difference in the world, and has become an advocate for labour rights. This should come as a relief. He is an intelligent young man and a persuasive speaker with a comprehensive knowledge of political theory. Had he remained with the far-Right, he could have employed those skills to become a potent propaganda tool and recruiter – or even a leader – for the movement.

That's not to say Cytanovic isn't ultimately responsible for his own actions. It's essential that he recognises the consequences of those actions will be long-lasting; making amends for harm done is a lifetime's commitment. But there also must be opportunities for atonement, whether that be through state-assisted volunteering programmes or community initiatives like Groundswell. Because if we deny people the chance to try being better, we risk perpetuating the cycle of extremism.

19 April 2022

The above information is reprinted with kind permission from UnHerd.
© 2023 UnHerd

www.unherd.com

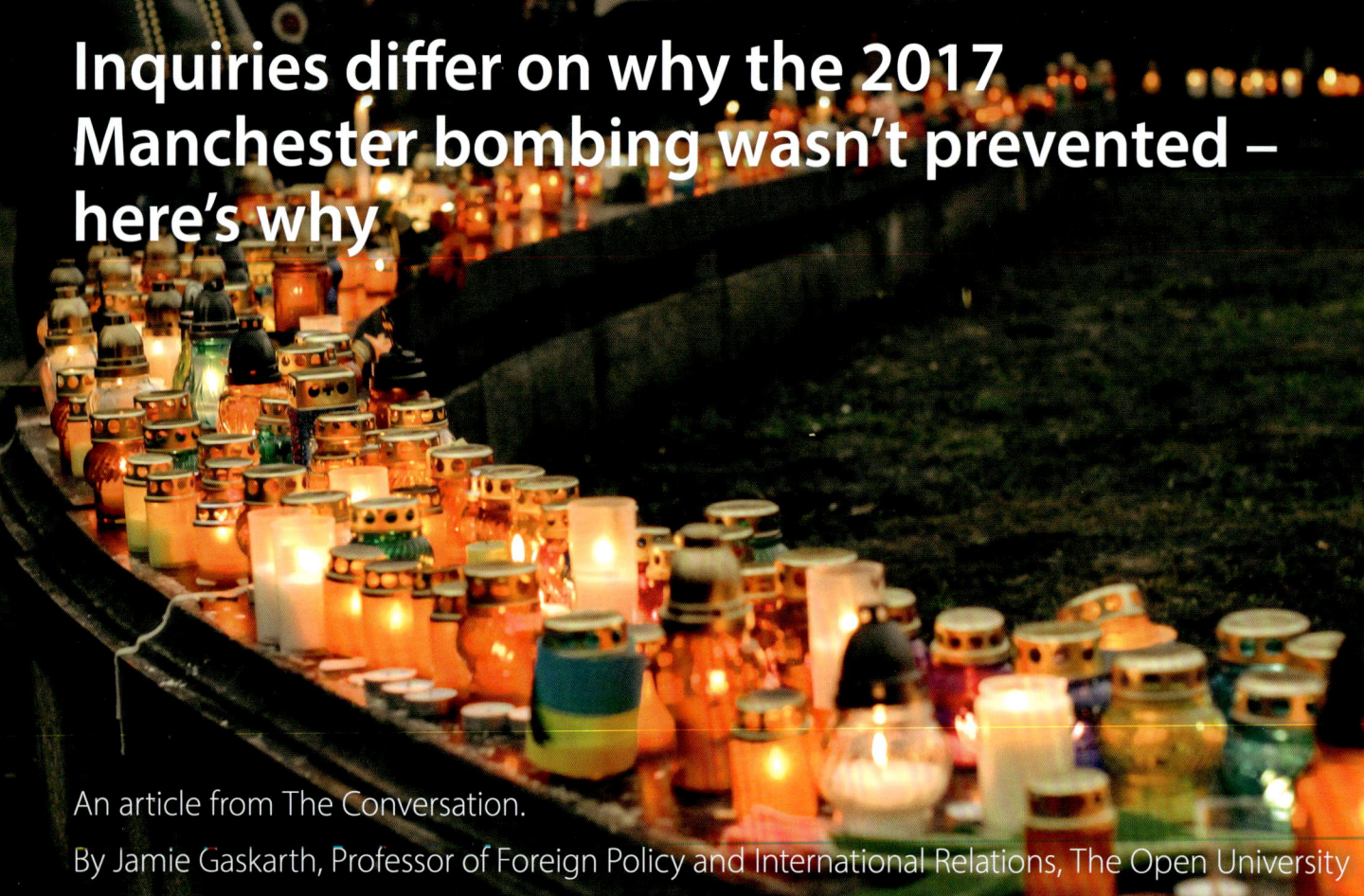

Inquiries differ on why the 2017 Manchester bombing wasn't prevented – here's why

An article from The Conversation.

By Jamie Gaskarth, Professor of Foreign Policy and International Relations, The Open University

How can you hold the intelligence and security services accountable, when what they do is secret? The third and final report from the public inquiry into the 2017 Manchester arena bombing is a useful guide.

Sir John Saunders, the retired judge in charge of the inquiry, has given a damning verdict on how government agencies handled the case of Salman Abedi, the man who set off a bomb at an Ariana Grande concert. His conclusions differed significantly from earlier reviews and the reasons why are important.

Abedi had been known to the authorities for years before he went on to kill 22 people and injure over 800 more. So the question must be why he was not prevented from carrying out the atrocity. Saunders highlighted individual failings that other reviews appear to have missed.

Past reports

There have been multiple investigations into the Manchester attack. The security service (MI5) and counter-terrorism police reviewed their own work soon after the atrocity. Further investigations were carried out by David Anderson, the former independent reviewer of terrorism legislation, and parliament's Intelligence and Security Committee.

These reports noted that officials could have made different decisions and recommended various actions to change future practice. The Intelligence and Security Committee argued that Abedi should have been referred to Prevent, the government's deradicalisation programme.

Anderson suggested the decision to end his designation as a 'subject of interest' – which would have involved more intense investigation – was wrong but ultimately concluded the mistake was understandable. The failure to thwart the attack was portrayed as a matter of bad luck. Anderson concluded: 'MI5 and CT [counter-terrorism] Policing got a great deal right ... they could have succeeded had the cards fallen differently.'

Such conclusions are typical of many reviews of the intelligence and security agencies. Too often, failures are portrayed as largely down to chance, the difficulties of intelligence gathering are emphasised, and individual mistakes are glossed over.

Saunders gives a very different version of events and it's important to understand how that came about. A key difference lies in the evidence Saunders gathered. Previous reviews relied upon accounts from senior figures, summarising the position of their organisations from a high level. By contrast, the Saunders inquiry interviewed junior officers, the people actually making decisions on the ground. Their perspective differed significantly.

Who gives evidence?

In his 2017 review, Anderson had accepted MI5's narrative that intelligence related to Abedi was mistakenly 'interpreted

... as to do probably with drugs or organised crime and not something to do with terrorism or national security'. After interviewing the relevant officers, Saunders disagreed, saying: 'I do not consider that these statements present an accurate picture.'

He found that officers had identified two pieces of intelligence about Abedi which were of concern on national security grounds. The first was not shared with counter-terrorism police. The second was not dealt with promptly.

As Saunders puts it, the officer reviewing the intelligence 'should have discussed it with other Security Service officers straight away. Moreover, s/he should have written the report on the same day, but in fact did not do so.' Furthermore, the report the officer produced on the second piece of intelligence was said to lack sufficient context.

Meanwhile, Abedi had collected material for the bomb and stored it in a car, where it sat for over a month while he travelled to Libya (presumably for training on preparing the device). Although there is no certainty about what difference these errors made, Saunders argues that had security services followed Abedi to the car, the bombing might have been prevented.

As such, individual as well as systemic failings were in play. What this underscores is the need to speak to officials at all levels of these agencies.

Identifying failures is not scapegoating

Senior officials can give a useful sense of the overall environment in which decisions are made. One witness for the inquiry notes that at the time they were running around 500 investigations into Islamist terrorism, about 3,000 people were designated subjects of interest and 40,000 were closed subjects. This context should be borne in mind but we now know that errors of judgement were made by individuals and addressing these is important.

Organisations can learn from individual mistakes. Was the officer who failed to share vital information underperforming across the board and it wasn't picked up? Did they wrongly interpret guidance? Were there personal or interpersonal issues affecting their decisions?

Were they overstretched? How did the individual and their managers respond when errors came to light? The answers to these questions could have vital implications for recruitment, training, operational decision making and management.

For too long apportioning blame has been associated with scapegoating. In reality, people doing immensely challenging jobs will make errors. GPs, surgeons, social workers, police officers, regularly have to make decisions with potentially life-changing consequences. Intelligence and security agencies are no different.

The Saunders inquiry underscores the need for oversight bodies like the Intelligence and Security Committee, as well as ad-hoc reviews, to be able to speak freely with all those involved, including frontline officers, so as to gain a full picture of what happened and how they can learn for the future.

3 March 2023

THE CONVERSATION

The above information is reprinted with kind permission from The Conversation.
© 2010-2023, The Conversation Trust (UK) Limited

www.theconversation.com

Further Reading/ Useful Websites

Useful Websites

www.bylinetimes.com

www.capx.co

www.gov.uk

www.independent.co.uk

www.inews.co.uk

www.metro.co.uk

www.news.un.org

www.politico.com

www.telegraph.co.uk

www.theconversation.com

www.theguardian.com

www.unherd.com

www.visionofhumanity.org

www.weforum.org

www.yougov.co.uk

Pages 3-5: Institute for Economics & Peace. *Global Terrorism Index 2022: Measuring the Impact of Terrorism, Sydney, March 2022.* Available from http://visionofhumanity.org/resources

Page 32: From UN News, by Peace and Security, ©(2023) United Nations. Reprinted with the permission of the United Nations. URL: https://news.un.org/en/story/2022/10/1130007. Date accessed 25/1/2023

Far Out: Encounters with Extremists by Charlotte McDonald Gibson (2022)

Coming of Age in the War on Terror by Randa Abdel-Fattah (2021)

Going Dark: The Secret Social Lives of Extremists by Julia Ebner (2021)

I Am Malala: The Girl Who Stood Up For Education and Was Shot by the Taliban by Malala Yousafzai with Christina Lamb (2013)

My Sister Lives on the Mantelpiece by Annabel Pitcher (2011)

The Looming Tower: Al Qaeda's Road to 9/11 by Lawrence Wright (2007)

Glossary

Al-Qaeda
A group/organisation of Islamic militants, responsible for the 9/11 attacks in America.

Al-Shabaab
Al-Shabaab is a terror group based in Somalia seeking to establish a fundamentalist Islamic state and imposing its strict version of sharia across East Africa.

CONTEST
Contest is the UK's counter-terrorism strategy aimed at reducing the risk to the UK and its citizens from terrorism.

Counter-terrorism
Counter-terrorism refers to the tactics and techniques used by governments and other groups to prevent or minimise a terrorist threat.

Cyber-terrorism
Also known as 'digital terrorism', is the attack by recognised terrorist groups against computer systems, causing maximum disruption.

Extremism
Extremism refers to beliefs or practices that are seen as radical, and can give rise to militance (e.g. groups justifying their violence on Islamic grounds, such as Al-Qaeda).

Global Terrorism Index (GTI)
An annual report published by the Institute for Economics and Peace ranking countries of the world according to their terrorist activity.

Ideology
An ideology is a system of cultural or political beliefs held by a group or individual.

Incel
An Incel or, involuntary celibate, is an individual (usually male) who blames women and society for their inability to find a romantic partner.

JNIM (Jama'at Nasr al-Islam wal Muslim)
JNIM was formed in 2017 and is a coalition of several jihadist groups in the Sahel. Its goal is for the entire region to be ruled under sharia law.

Radicalisation
The process by which a person, or group of people, adopt extreme religious, political or ideological beliefs.

Sahel
The Sahel is a 5,000 kilometre area of land below the Sahara Desert that stretches from Africa's Atlantic coast to the Red Sea.

Terrorism
The word 'terrorism' dates back to the 18th century, but there is no globally accepted definition of the term. The most widely accepted is probably that put forward by the US State Department, which states that terrorism is 'premeditated, politically motivated violence perpetrated against non-combatant targets by subnational groups or clandestine agents, usually intended to influence an audience.' Types include Nationalist-Separatist, Religious, Right-Wing and Left-Wing Terrorism.

The Taliban
A fundamentalist Islamist group which ruled large parts of Afghanistan between 1996 and 2001 when it was ousted by US forces. It returned to power in 2021.

Violent extremism
When violence is used to achieve or promote radical/extreme religious, political or ideological beliefs.

Index

A
adultification 1
Afghanistan 33–34
al-Qaeda 33–34, 43
al-Shabaab 5, 34, 36, 43

B
Begum, Shamima 1–2, 14–15
bomb-making 1
Brexit 7
British values 20

C
censorship 32
Channel programmes 11
Climo, Conor 22–24
Commission for Countering Extremism 1, 20
CONTEST strategy 2018 27, 43
    see also counter-terrorism
Copeland, David 19
counter-terrorism 10–12, 16–17, 21, 26–27, 32–33, 40
Cox, Jo 19
Crime and Disorder Act 1998 21
Criminal Justice Act 2003 21
cyber terrorism 5, 43
Cytanovic, Peter 38–39

D
Davies, Alex 19
Davison, Jake 16
Delhi Declaration 31
Dymock, Andrew 10

E
extremism 1, 6–8, 16, 20–21, 27, 36, 43

F
far-Right terrorism 2, 10, 38–39
Feuerkrieg Division (FKD) 22–23
forgiveness 38–39

G
Global Peace Index 2022 36
Global Terrorism Index 2022 3–5, 36, 43

H
human rights 31–32
Human Rights Act, Article 8 31

I
ideologies 6–7, 16, 43
incels 16, 43
Independent Reviewer of Terrorism Legislation 16–17
Institute of Economics and Peace (IEP) 3
intercultural dialogues 36–37
Irish Republican extremists 8
ISIS 1
Islamic extremists 8
Islamic State (IS) 5
Islamist extremism 33
Islamophobia 20–21, 25–26

J
jihadism 1–2
JNIM (Jama'at Nasr al-Islam wal Muslim) 5, 43

L
Leak, Andrew 25
left wing extremism 8–9
legislation 1, 17, 21, 27, 29
liberal-left 2
lone actors 18–19

M
Manchester bombing 2017 40–41
misogyny 16–17
Morrice, Dean 19
Muslim experiences 12–13
Muslim militants 2

N
National Action 19
neo-Nazi terrorism 10, 16–17, 19, 22–23, 38–39
Netpol 21

O
online radicalisation 28, 35

P
political violence 2, 4, 8–9
politicisation, of terrorism 2
POLITICO 22
populism 7
Prevent 11, 27
prison 10, 31
propaganda 21, 29
psychology of extremism 6–7

R
Racial and Religious Hatred Act 2006 21
racism, and intelligence 7
radicalisation 1, 11, 21, 27–28, 31, 35, 43
religious violence 4, 12–13
right wing extremism 8–10, 11, 18–19
Rushdie, Salman 21

S
Sahel 3–4, 43
social media 1
Sub-Saharan Africa, deaths from terrorism 3
Syria 1–2, 14–15

T
Taliban 5, 34, 43
terrorism, definition 43
Terrorism Act 2000 17, 19, 21, 27
Trump, Donald 6–7, 38–39

U
Ukraine conflict 5
United States, Capitol storming 6–7
Unite the Right rally 16, 38–39

W
working classes 10